SO INNOCENT,

YET

SO DEAD

Written By

Bill Davis

A police detective who investigated the crime.

Coastal Winds Publishing House
Port Arthur, Texas

Coastal Winds Publishing House
3167 63rd Street
Port Arthur, Texas 77640

ISBN: 978-0-9850403-8-3
Library of Congress Control Number: 2016935026

Cover design and layout by:
Gail C. Jenkins of Caring Hearts Publishing and
Pamela Joy Licatino of SeaShore Creations by Design.

THIS BOOK WAS WRITTEN
IN SPECIAL MEMORY OF

Falyssa Van Winkle

May her memory

and the memory of

so many others like her

never die.

May the courage of survivors,

like the late Lucille Jackson

forever stand tall,

against the aggressors of evil.

SPECIAL THANKS

I would like to extend special thanks to Falyssa's mom and step-dad, Elaine and Joe Langley. Elaine provided all of Falyssa's photographs, along with countless details, and supported fully the telling of her daughter's story.

I would like to extend special thanks to Mrs. Lucille Jackson's daughter, Myrna Cooley, for providing photographs and details of her mother's life.

ACKNOWLEDGEMENTS

As with any undertaking of this magnitude, there are always so many wonderful people to thank, but my first acknowledgement of gratitude is to God. I firmly believe that the idea for this book came from Him. Through His Grace came the fortitude and perseverance to accomplish this task. I hope and pray that His will has been done and that He receives the honor and glory for this endeavor. Now with His blessing, this book has sold over 35,000 copies and is in its second printing.

I would like to say a special "Thank You" to my beautiful and beloved wife, Mary. She has taught me the true meaning of love. Her help, encouragement, and assistance have enabled me to multiply my speaking engagements throughout the country, trying to save children from abuse, neglect, and molestation. She is truly my wife, my help mate, my soul mate, my love, and my best friend.

I owe a special thanks to my son, Dusty Davis. He spent many hours sticking bar code stickers on the back cover of thousands of books in the first printing. He also had to stamp the ISBN number on the inside cover of those same books.

To my Mom, Nevada W. Davis, and my Dad, the late Carl Davis: thanks for instilling within me a love for God, high moral values, and the initiative to succeed. To Pat and Johnny Long, my surrogate parents: thanks for sustaining those high ideals and being there for me through the years.

I am so proud and honored to belong to the greatest fraternity in the world - the men and women in "Blue" who put their lives on the line every day. A special note of gratitude goes to the late

Sgt. Bill Tatum, my friend and fellow investigator on this case. He was a wonderful Christian man, husband, father, grandfather, and police officer. He is sorely missed.

This book could not have been written without the assistance of two Newton County Officials, Sheriff Wayne Powell and District Clerk Abbie Nell Stark. All of the crime scene photographs, trial transcripts and court file materials were provided by Newton County, and special thanks go to Deputy District Clerk Karyn for her assistance in compiling and authenticating these voluminous documents. Also, Wayne Powell's Chief Deputy Ricky Hillin, Captain Belinda Sills, and Reserve Deputy Danny Dowden must be acknowledged for helping me obtain further documentation to make this book as factually complete as possible.

To Ms. Charlotte Parry: Thank you so much for many hours of critiquing my book and for the poem. This book would not have been the same without your help, for the special place you have in your heart for victims, and for your special prayers.

Similar thanks go to Ms. Glenda Peacock of Lumberton High School: without your red marks on my manuscript, this book might never have been published.

I must admit that my knowledge of computers doesn't go much past turning one on. Several people helped me in spite of my electronic inexperience. Pat O'Quinn, Danny Martinez and Lynda West helped me over the computer hurdles and had infinite patience with this novice author.

To Dr. Vic Sims, former professor at the Lamar University Criminal Justice Department: You told me to quit worrying about all of the little technicalities and "just write it." Thanks for the advice and encouragement; I took it, and I did it!

And to my special friends, Kay Williams and Freddie Bobb: Thanks for countless prayers and for lifting me up when I was down. I would also like to thank my Pastor, Ralph Martin, and so many others at Grace Church who have continuously kept me in their prayers. Don't stop.

And then there is my friend and a wonderful lady named Gail Jenkins, who saw my dreams, removed the stumbling blocks, and allowed my manuscript to be published. Without her enthusiasm and resources, my book would probably still be stuck in some publisher's office in New York City. She helped edit the final manuscript, select photographs, and design the layout of the book and its cover (while trying to run her law practice).

Cynthia Simon cannot be thanked enough for her countless hours to get my manuscript ready for print. I know that my lack of computer knowledge tested her nerves to the end. Words cannot express my thanks to each of you. In the final days, Gail and Cynthia worked virtually around the clock to meet the publishing deadline, and they cheered up this author when the task seemed impossible. God sent a host of angels my way when you appeared.

There is no doubt that my prayers were answered when Gail Jenkins found our final editor, Maribeth Jones. She worked under an impossible timetable to make this book a reality. Her parents did not waste their money in sending Maribeth to journalism school!

My friend, George Lavergne with Triangle Blueprint, Inc. has always believed in me and my projects. He undertook the printing of this book with interest and zeal because he knew Falyssa's story needed to be told.

A special thanks goes out to Ellen Baber, George's employee.

She took my additions and edits for the book's second printing and made it a reality. Ellen also makes sure that I always have enough child abuse booklets, children's coloring books, and brochures when I'm getting ready to present a seminar or speak at a conference.

Thanks to so many others I am failing to mention: you know who you are. I will always be indebted to you for your encouragement and prayers. All of you kept me going and helped make this book possible.

Bill Davis

FOREWARD

I never met Falyssa Van Winkle. The first time I heard her name was the day she was murdered, but her tragedy has haunted me since that moment. From everything I have been told, she was a warm, loving little girl who was full of life. I wish I had met her. Through my research and the pictures furnished by her mother, I feel I knew her well.

Parents strive to raise their children in a warm, loving environment. They believe their children will grow into adulthood and live rewarding lives. Most children do. But occasionally a perverted individual snuffs out a precious little life, leaving a family and community to ask, "Why?"

On October 6, 1990, Falyssa Van Winkle became a statistic. I have pictured the horrible scene countless times - a 10-year-old girl lying gagged on the floor of a motor home. I have pictured tears rolling down her cheeks as she experienced the excruciating pain of rape at the hands of this human animal. Most of all, I have never been able to erase the image of Falyssa's eyes and face as she desperately tried to breathe while her attacker tightened the rope around her neck. I determined then that for me, Falyssa would not be just another statistic.

I had another motive for writing this book - to increase public awareness of crimes like this one. Many times our communities, our civic leaders, and the media do not realize that countless numbers of children are sexually molested each and every day in our society. Often the attacker is no stranger to the victim or the family. Some incidents are never reported. Others are reported to the authorities but not always the public.

This book was written as a memorial to Falyssa Van Winkle - a precious, vivacious little girl. It was also written on behalf of countless other victims of rape and sexual molestation. I hope each of them can live not just as a victim, but as a survivor.

TABLE OF CONTENTS

LEGEND OF MAIN CHARACTERS
(IN ALPHABETICAL ORDER)

BEN BAKER
Assistant Defense Attorney for Rex Powell

BILL DAVIS
Beaumont Police Department, Sex Crimes Investigator

LOUIS DUGAS
Lead Defense Attorney for Rex Powell

JUDGE JOE BOB GOLDEN
State District Judge presided over Rex Powell's 1991 trial

LUCILLE JACKSON
A victim of Rex Powell in 1984 in Merryville, Louisiana

ELAINE & JOE LANGLEY
Mother and stepfather of Falyssa Van Winkle

PAUL McWILLIAMS
Chief prosecutor for Jefferson County, Texas, District Attorney's Office, helped prosecute the 1991 trial.

CHARLES MITCHELL
Former Newton County, Texas, District Attorney, prosecuted the 1991 trial.

CORLISS POWELL
Wife of defendant, Rex Powell

JAMES REXFORD "REX" POWELL
Defendant

SHERIFF WAYNE POWELL
(Not Related to Defendant)
Sheriff of Newton County, Texas

A SPECIAL TRIBUTE
(to Falyssa)

Her smile was like the sunshine,
So warm, so bright, so alive.
Her tender innocence came shining through
Each time you looked into her eyes.

To be a part of her world
Was to know an all consuming love.
She was as bright as the brightest star
That shines in the Heavens above.
Although a monster snuffed out her light,
Her memory fills our heads.
This sweet and precious gift from God,
So innocent, yet so dead!

Written by
CHAROLETTE PARRY
1993

PROLOGUE: THE BRIDGE

It had just stopped raining in southern Newton County, Texas, on October 6, 1990 -- one of those early afternoon East Texas thunderstorms lasting just about thirty minutes but assuring that the rest of the day would be unbearably humid.

David and Sandra Cassalias decided they would take a break from working on the zoo and recreational area they were developing. Their fish pond had been dug but needed more stock, so they decided to seine for small fish at Cow Creek on Hwy. 1416, a quarter-mile east of Hwy. 87. On their all-terrain vehicle, the Cassalias couple rode to Cow Creek Bridge, crossed it and took the trail down the north embankment. David drove to a mud hole, now filled with water from the afternoon rain. As he turned back toward the bridge, he saw something he would never forget -- not thirty feet away, lying face down in a puddle of water was the clothed body of a child. He moved to within eight or ten feet of the lifeless form. Sandra also saw the body as she moved in behind David. The word accident never entered their minds, only murder. Who could have done this? Where was the killer? Was he hiding in the bushes watching them at this very moment? David drove up the south embankment, made a U-turn, crossed the bridge, and sped toward home. Once there, he jumped into his truck and drove to see his nearest neighbor, who happened to be in law enforcement.

R.D. Cox was enjoying his Saturday off, watching television in the coolness of his living room. A twenty-one-year veteran trooper with the Texas Department of Public Safety, R.D. questioned David. Though he didn't want to believe the gruesome story, R.D. was a seasoned cop who had developed a sixth sense. He had come to rely on that sixth sense to tell him when someone was telling the truth. R.D. felt this story was true, just as sure as he knew it was Saturday. He jumped into his patrol car and followed David to the bridge.

Sandra had beat them back to the scene with her father and two local high school boys who worked for her and David. R.D. approached the small body. The face was immersed in water and mud. He checked for a pulse but knew there would be none. Lifting the head from the water, he discovered that the body was of a young girl with a rope around her neck.

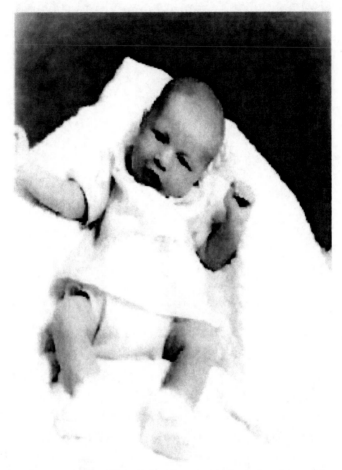

Falyssa Van Winkle's first photograph, nine days old

CHAPTER ONE

OLD TIME TRADE DAYS

Larry's Antique Mall was one of Southeast Texas' most interesting places to visit in 1990. Located in Beaumont, a city of 125,000 and about ninety miles east of Houston, Larry's was open every Saturday and Sunday, attracting people throughout the area who came to browse through its various shops, craft booths and antiques.

The weekend following the first Monday of the month was known far and wide as Old Time Trade Days. The mall drew about 250 to 500 vendors from all over the United States, who set up to sell or trade their wares to the thousands of visitors and Trade Days "regulars."

Larry's was owned and operated by Larry and Justine Tinkle, lifelong residents of Beaumont. The building that housed Larry's Antique Mall was built in 1949, and originally housed a hardware store, one of several hardware stores in the Tinkle chain. Larry and Justine bought the store from the family in 1969 and operated it as Larry's Hardware Store until 1975. The building's size and location prompted churches and other organizations to ask for permission to hold antique sales and flea markets on the property. By this time, Eastex Freeway had opened and the building was now becoming an insurance liability as it sat vacant.

One day, as Justine and Larry were clearing out items that had been left behind by flea markets, they discovered several antique items. They called friends who were interested in antiques, and the idea to open an antique mall was born. The idea grew to include Old Time Trade Days, fashioned after the Canton Flea Market in Canton, Texas, and known as the largest flea market in the world. Since Larry's Old Time Trade Days was held on the weekend after "First Monday" trade days in Canton, it wasn't long before a parade of vendors in Canton began loading their wares and traveling to Beaumont to wait for the weekend to arrive.

On Saturday, October 6, 1990, Old Time Trade Days was in fullswing. The vendors were set up all around the expansive Antique Mall building. The hot sun was bright in a cloudless sky and the temperature was in the high 80's, uncharacteristically warm for October.

Larry was scurrying around the grounds tending to the minor maintenance. Just the day before, he'd had to dig trenches to drain standing water left by afternoon thunderstorms the week before. Since early that morning, Justine had been busy with newspaper reporter David Bauerlien from the *Beaumont Enterprise*. Larry and Justine had been trying to change a city zoning ordinance to allow greater expansion on their property for Old Time Trade Days. They were met with resistance from several members of the Beaumont City Council who feared expansion would bring parking and noise problems. Justine was doing her best to tell her side of the story to Bauerlien while tending to her desk and the phones inside the mall building.

About 11:00 a.m., vendor Elaine Langley from nearby Lake Charles, Louisiana, came to Justine's desk looking for her ten-year-old daughter, Falyssa. Justine's granddaughter, Bunnye, and Falyssa were close friends and usually ran around together during Old Time Trade Days. Elaine thought the two girls might be together, but Bunnye had not seen Falyssa. Justine paged Falyssa. She knew that the child would know to come to her desk in the main building. Elaine left and continues to search for her daughter. Justine went back to dealing with the day's tasks and the ever-present newspaper reporter who had endless questions.

Since she could not leave her desk to look for Falyssa, Justine sent Bunnye to look in all the restrooms in the main building in case she had been in one of them and had not heard the page. Justine then sent Bunnye onto the grounds to check with various vendors who knew Falyssa to see if they knew her whereabouts.

About twenty minutes later, Elaine returned to Justine's desk. Anyone looking at her could plainly see she was concerned. Falyssa never went anywhere alone without asking permission from her mother or step-father, Joe. Even then, Falyssa checked back with them every thirty minutes or so. There was no doubt about it; she'd been gone too long. When Justine discovered that Elaine had not found Falyssa, she began paging the child every few minutes. Larry heard the pages and came to the desk to see what was wrong. Learning that Falyssa could not be found, Larry went out onto the grounds to look for her. Several vendors joined the search. By now it was noon, and Falyssa had not been seen for about two hours.

The search continued throughout the afternoon. As word of the child's disappearance spread, everyone at Larry's Antique Mall was becoming frantic. Several vendors locked up their wares early to look for Falyssa.

About a mile south of Larry's Antique Mall on the opposite side of Hwy. 69 (Eastex Freeway) was the sprawling Parkdale Mall. Although Elaine and Joe were certain Falyssa would not have gone there, concerned vendors photocopied pictures of Falyssa that Elaine kept in her purse and circulated them throughout Parkdale Mall. No one at the mall had seen Falyssa.

Typically, Old Time Trade Days were fun-filled times where families and friends came to browse and visit. On October 6, 1990, it became a parent's worst nightmare for the Langleys. The events of this day would soon cause thousands of other parents to not let their children out of their sight, even in familiar settings.

The main building at Larry's Antique Mall
as it appeared in 1990.

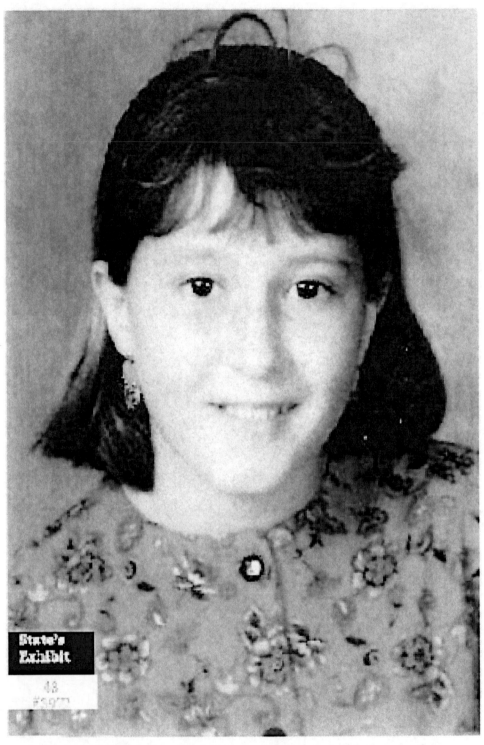

Falyssa's sixth-grade school picture, taken days before her death.

CHAPTER TWO

FALYSSA DISAPPEARS

Joe Langley and Elaine Van Winkle were married on December 14, 1985. Elaine had two daughters from a previous marriage -- Shonna, born April 16, 1977, and Falyssa, born December 14, 1979. Elaine's mother remembered Falyssa's joy when Elaine and Joe decided to tie the knot on the child's sixth birthday. For Falyssa, it was the best birthday present of all.

Falyssa was a normal yet unique little girl. Very extroverted, she was a leader, not a follower. She performed in every one of her class plays from kindergarten through fifth grade. She loved taking French and was accomplished at speaking and writing the language. She did well in her other classes also, always making the A/B Honor Roll.

Falyssa loved animals and the outdoors. Otherwise "mean" neighborhood dogs took a liking to her as if they could sense her caring nature. During the hot months, Falyssa loved to play outside wearing her favorite one-piece romper suits. She was sad when she outgrew them during her fourth-grade year.

In 1990, Falyssa was not only developing intellectually and physically, but socially. In sixth grade she met her first boyfriend, Chris. He was a year older, but Falyssa was two to three inches taller. The weekend before the Langleys went to Old Time Trade Days, Falyssa and Chris went on a "date" to the movies, accompanied by Elaine and Chris's mother, Teressa; his sister Marlena, who was also Falyssa's best friend; and his older brother Mike. The two families went to see "Ghost," in which a murdered man returns to his wife in spirit to avenge his killer.

As they were exiting the theater, Falyssa turned to her mother and said, "Mom, if anyone killed me, I'd definitely show you who did it." Elaine thought that was an odd statement, then stored her daughter's comment in the back of her mind as they left the theater parking lot.

Chris and Falyssa had entered into a new era in their lives -- adolescence. Already, the two planned their second date to a school dance the Friday after Old Time Trade Days. Chris had bought Falyssa a gold necklace with a cultured pearl pendant, and a pin that spelled "LOVE" under a rainbow.

Elaine had always enjoyed making crafts and visiting craft shows. She was very accomplished at restoring carousel horses, tole painting, t-shirt painting, and making costumes and Barbie clothes for her daughter. She operated a booth at numerous craft shows. Elaine's dad, Martin Lavergne, and her step-mother, Lola, also loved going to flea markets and antique malls -- especially to Canton and Old Time Trade Days at Larry's.

Martin and Lola first took Joe and Elaine to Larry's Old Time Trade Days in 1988. Soon, the Langleys decided to set up their own booth. Joe had just begun working with collectibles, but Elaine had been dabbling with them for years. Setting up a booth seemed like a profitable way to share their hobby. Their first booth opened at Larry's in 1989.

On Friday afternoon, October 5, 1990, Elaine and Falyssa left Lake Charles and headed west on IH-10 for the one-hour drive to Beaumont and Larry's Antique Mall where Joe was busy getting ready.

Elaine and Falyssa arrived at Larry's and visited with their vendor friends until after dark. Falyssa had already gone inside their trailer, and after her parents watched the news, they retired for the evening. Falyssa settled down to sleep with her pink "snow baby" doll she received from her grandmother, Carol Van Winkle, for her second Christmas. The doll had only one eye and a few of the fingers had been chewed off by a family cat, but it still played the song Falyssa had grown to love more than any other -- "It's A Small World." As the doll played its song for her that last time, she drifted into a peaceful night's sleep.

Even though it was autumn, Saturday was going to be another

hot Southeast Texas day for Old Time Trade Days. Being a typical ten-year-old, Falyssa slept late. Elaine woke her to tell her that their good friends, Larry and Patricia Aikins, were there. She asked her daughter if she wanted to accompany them to nearby Vidor to browse a flea market. Well, naturally, it's more fun to watch Saturday morning cartoons or to walk around Larry's with your own friends than to tag along with grownups while they browse at more booths. So Falyssa decided to stay at Larry's. Elaine told her that Joe would be right outside the camper if she needed anything. As always, the family made sure they knew where everyone was.

When Falyssa finally came out of their trailer she was hungry for breakfast. Joe told her where to find the cereal but she came right back out because the Langleys had forgotten to buy milk. Regardless, Falyssa ate the dry cereal as she and her step-father began their day together. In a few minutes, a man Joe knew only as the "Mayor of Mauriceville" stopped by to visit. He was Rex Powell, who had given himself the nickname for reasons no one knew. He wasn't a close friend, just one of many acquaintances, like so many others, that Falyssa and her parents saw once a month. Joe and his family had known the "Mayor" for about a year, seeing him off and on at the flea market. Falyssa said hello to Rex, then said she had something to show him. She went back inside the trailer and returned with her photo album. She was so proud of her new boyfriend! With great pride, she showed Rex the photo of Chris. Joe noticed a strange look pass across Rex's face. It was a despondent look, like he had just been reminded of a sad memory.

The sky darkened and it started raining. Falyssa, Joe, and Rex visited a few more minutes. When the rain stopped, Rex said goodbye and walked on, continuing to browse. Joe had several customers waiting, so Falyssa went back inside the trailer.

Elaine and Jane returned from their Vidor trip about an hour later. When they got to the Langley booth, Falyssa was inside the trailer sipping on a glass of Gatorade. Elaine stuck her head in the door to let her daughter know she was back. Elaine went outside and Falyssa followed her a few minutes later.

Joe, Elaine, and Larry, their vendor neighbor, were eating peanuts. Falyssa sat in her mom's lap, hugging on her, when she asked, "Daddy, can I have a dollar for a bag of peanuts?" Joe gave her a dollar and promised her that he would pay her the rest of her $5 allowance later in the day after they made some sales at the booth. Falyssa hugged her mom, kissed her on the neck, and said, "I love you, Mom." Elaine responded with her own hug and kiss and told Falyssa, "I love you too."

As Falyssa headed for the peanut stand, an intense, cold feeling came over Elaine. She started to get up to go with her daughter, but couldn't seem to get out of the chair. She dismissed her feelings as strange. What nonsense to have such weird thoughts! After all, people were everywhere. What could happen in such a busy, family-centered place like Larry's during Old Time Trade Days?

CHAPTER THREE

THE INVESTIGATION BEGINS

Sgt. Curtis Whittaker of the Newton County Sheriff's Office was preparing to go on evening patrol. He wondered if this evening would be another busy October Saturday night with the typical family disturbances, bar room brawls and auto collisions. He stopped and visited with dispatcher, Brenda Seal, when the radio suddenly crackled with a voice Whittaker recognized as State Trooper R.D. Cox. The sound of R.D.'s voice told Whittaker that something was very wrong. "I need you and the sheriff to come to Cow Creek Bridge on Hwy. 1416. We have a body under the bridge. Get here right away."

Whittaker quickly left the sheriff's department office and drove south on Hwy. 87, pressing his patrol car to its limit. Seal called Sheriff Powell. Whittaker made the eighteen-mile trip in ten minutes, arriving to see several people gathered at the bridge. Cox took Whittaker to the body of the little girl. Whittaker would later state in his report: "Juvenile subject was face down in a puddle of water. The water came up above the ears on the victim as she lay in the mud hole. The victim was lying with her head to the south and her feet to the north."

Whittaker met David and Sandra Cassalias. They told him why they were under the bridge and when they had discovered the young girl's body.

Justice of the Peace Walter Fortenberry arrived at the bridge a short time later and pronounced the little girl dead. He contacted Stringer Funeral Home in Kirbyville to come and take charge of the body. Whittaker, Cox and Judge Fortenberry examined the body closer, focusing on the piece of cotton rope tied around the little girl's neck. As they rolled her body to the side, they saw that her wrists were bound with similar rope.

Good investigative technique at a crime scene search requires "searching out" from the point of origin in ever-widening circles.

About eight and one-half feet from the victim's right foot officers found three more pieces of rope similar to the rope around the little girl's neck and wrists. These pieces were hanging on bushes and strewn on the ground as if thrown there. Was it coincidental that these pieces of rope happened to be in the immediate vicinity? Or, had the perpetrator tossed away extra rope so that if ever questioned, this item of evidence could not be linked to him?

Sheriff Powell and his wife Joy were headed to dinner in Jasper when Seal radioed for Unit #1. Seal told the sheriff about the little girl found under the bridge, adding that the preliminary investigation showed she may have been hanged. The sheriff turned his car around and headed back to Newton. He ran inside his office and grabbed his video camera, feeling that this was not any ordinary homicide. Somehow he knew that he was going to need every investigative technique and tool at his disposal to solve this case. That included friend and fellow officer, Texas Ranger Ron McBride.

McBride is a Texas Ranger stationed in Beaumont with the primary assignment of working with law enforcement agencies throughout East Texas. McBride was raised in the Newton County area, and he agreed to rush to the scene. The sheriff headed south on Hwy. 87 toward Cow Creek Bridge.

Sheriff Powell went to the little girl's body and began gathering information from Whittaker and Cox. Joy Powell stood back in the crowd of civilians that had grown to about twenty people. She had been a nurse for many years and had seen just about everything imaginable that could be done to a human body. But when the body is a child, one never gets used to it.

Ranger McBride arrived at the scene within a matter of minutes. An array of law enforcement officers were gathered at the bridge trying to piece together this deadly puzzle. One end of the rope that was knotted around the little girl's neck was three-feet-long leading to the theory that she had been hanged. But from where? The top of the bridge? The puddle she was lying in was under the bridge by only a couple of feet. She could have been forced over the edge, held by the end of the rope until death occurred, then dropped into the muddy water below.

In the October 8, 1990 issue of *Beaumont Enterprise*, news of the murder was headlined "Killer Hanged Girl, Authorities Say." An unidentified spokeswoman for the Department of Public Safety was quoted as saying that the little girl had been hanged and then thrown in a puddle of water. However, the only Department of Public Safety spokespersons on the scene were R.D. Cox and Ron McBride, and they did not make any such representations. The horrible hanging theory later proved to be false.

Theories aside for now, neither the officers at the scene nor the civilians at the bridge knew the child. Powell began calling to the crime scene everyone he could think of who might know the girl -- store owners, school principals and teachers. No one could identify her.

There were so many people under the bridge by now that Powell feared evidence might be destroyed. He knew that the trail of a killer could be thrown off with the loss of a single footprint, trace of blood, or tire track. With Whittaker and Newton County Deputies Choyce Gandy and Ricky Hillin, Powell cleared the onlookers and began re-securing the crime scene to gather evidence. He brought out his new video camera and started filming the scene; however, he needed to attend to overseeing the investigation. Sandra Cassalias stepped in to lend her experience with the video camera. Powell instructed her as to what needed to be filmed. Meanwhile, precise measurements were taken of the body, the rope pieces and footprints found in the sand between the body and the creek. Investigators never know when a crime scene might have to be re-constructed, so accurate measurements are critical.

As work to secure the crime scene progressed, Powell again turned his attention to the child's identity. Who was this beautiful, innocent, forever-silenced little girl? He notified his dispatcher to get in touch with every law enforcement agency within a one-hundred-mile radius of Newton County to check for a missing person's report on a little girl matching the victim's description. She had to belong to someone. He knew that somewhere a mom and dad must be frantically worried, wondering what had happened to their young daughter.

Sgt. Bill Davis stands on the dirt road that leads to Hwy. 1416
to his left and under Cow Creek Bridge to his right.

Area under Cow Creek Bridge where Falyssa's body was found.

Sgt. Bill Davis pointing to Cow Creek Bridge.

Sgt. Bill Davis shows where Falyssa's body
was found face down in the water.

The question Sgt. Bill Davis and so many others ponder is,
"How anyone could have done this to such a beautiful little girl?"

Falyssa, age one, Christmas portrait taken
with sister, Shonna, in 1980.

CHAPTER FOUR

THE IDENTITY

Because of the conflict that Larry and Justine were having with Beaumont City Council over the zoning ordinance and parking problems surrounding Old Time Trade Days, they had hired off-duty uniformed Beaumont police officers to control parking in the front area. On the morning of October 6, 1990, Officer R.D. Anderson finished his midnight shift and went straight from the police station to Larry's to work. Just before he left at 1:00 p.m. he heard that a ten-year-old girl had disappeared from the property. Everyone felt that Falyssa would *surely* turn up sooner or later.

Officer J.B. Simonson arrived at Larry's to relieve Anderson. Within minutes, Elaine Langley found him and told him her daughter was missing. Simonson knew that in most cases like this the missing child is off playing with friends and time has just slipped away. From Elaine he got the first official description of the missing girl: white female, ten years old, five feet tall wearing a peach colored shorts set with an umbrella design on the shirt. Falyssa had now been missing for almost three hours.

Simonson began a methodical search. He walked the entire display area and searched the wooded perimeter of the antique mall. About this time, the same thunderstorm that had struck southern Newton County brought heavy rain to north Beaumont. Most of the customers called it a day and left Larry's. Vendors covered their wares to protect them from the downpour. Simonson got in his vehicle and continued to search as the rain fell. Nothing. Even with the rain, no Falyssa.

When the rain stopped, Elaine found Simonson and told him she wanted to file an official missing persons report. He gave Elaine a phone number that she thought was to the national missing children's hotline but in fact was the Beaumont Police Department. She was about to place a call that every parent hopes they never have to make.

Mae Eaglin, a clerical receptionist for the Beaumont Police Department, answered Elaine's call. Frantic, she told how her little girl had been missing for hours. Eaglin began to fill in the blanks on the report that would later be labeled Missing Persons Report #90-92637: Van Winkle, Falyssa.

Eaglin immediately entered the report into the National Crime Information Center (N.C.I.C.) and Texas Crime Information Center (T.C.I.C.) computer networks. Elaine did not know that by the time she made Falyssa's disappearance official, her daughter's body had already been discovered underneath Cow Creek Bridge and was awaiting identification.

For the next couple of hours, Elaine kept busy calling friends and relatives. She tried getting in touch with Falyssa's father, Michael Van Winkle, in Lake Charles. The line was continuously busy. She finally dialed the operator, only to discover that there were technical problems with the phone. Elaine called her cousin Lorna Lanier, also in Lake Charles, and asked Lorna to go to Michael's house to see if he had picked up Falyssa from Larry's without telling her. In her heart, Elaine knew Michael had not picked up Falyssa. But she was so upset she was following any and every suggestion to find her daughter.

Lorna went to the Van Winkle home and talked with Falyssa's stepmother, Julie. Falyssa had not been there and Michael was at work. Lorna called Elaine back with the news. Elaine's next call was to her dad, Martin Lavergne. She needed him with her. Martin assured his daughter that he would be on his way. Within minutes, Martin, his wife, Lola, and his son, Nelson, and his girlfriend, Karen, were headed west on IH-10 for the sixty-mile trip to Beaumont. When they arrived at Larry's at 7:15 p.m., Elaine threw her arms around her father for the much needed comfort and support that only a daddy can give in such terrible times. There had still been no word on Falyssa.

Meanwhile, Sheriff Powell's investigation was moving slowly. With everyone he had brought to the bridge to identify the little girl's body, he was still no closer than the first minute he had laid eyes on her. He was not in need of volunteers. In the meantime, word of the little body under the bridge quickly spread through the rural community.

At 6:30 p.m., the Department of Public Safety dispatcher working with investigators called the Beaumont Police Department for information on the department's recent missing white female juveniles. There was only one, and everything in the report matched the body of the deceased child under Cow Creek Bridge, eighty miles away. Official identification had not yet been made, but that was just a matter of time. Sheriff Powell knew he finally had a name to go with the child.

Always-fiesty Falyssa was mugging for the camera before sister Shonna gave her a pinch, resulting in this pose, taken in 1982.

CHAPTER FIVE

SATURDAY NIGHT -- REALITY SETS IN

If ever there was a sad mess, it was on Saturday night, October 6, 1990 in Newton County. Sheriff Powell was still under Cow Creek Bridge knowing that he was in charge of the murder investigation of a little girl. He had just learned the child's identity. Yet so many questions remained, with the most frustrating one being, who could do such an unthinkable thing?

As he searched all day for Falyssa, Joe Langley had a nagging feeling that the man he knew as Rex, the "Mayor of Mauriceville" might know something about the disappearance of his step-daughter. He couldn't forget the eerie look he'd seen on Rex's face that morning when Falyssa had shown him the photo of her little boyfriend. No one at Larry's knew Rex's last name, and Joe needed to talk to Rex to see if he might know something, anything.

Joe remembered that Rex had a booth on occasion at the Mauriceville Flea Market about thirty miles northeast of Beaumont. Joe got the owner's phone number from Justine and gave her a call. She did know a man who liked to refer to himself as the "Mayor of Mauriceville." His name was Rex Powell. After hearing about Falyssa, the woman assured Joe she would try to get Rex's phone number and call Joe back as soon as possible.

That evening at Beaumont police headquarters, Sgt. Curtis Breaux's first call was to Lt. Charles Tyler, supervisor of the detectives working crimes-against-persons cases. From the information Breaux relayed to him, Tyler knew this was going to be an extensive investigation. He instructed Breaux to call a roster of officers that included Lt. Melissa Ownby, supervisor of detectives who work crimes-against-property cases, and Sgt. Bill Jordan, a detective in the Youth Services Bureau. Jordan worked with juveniles who were in trouble with the law but he was also assigned reports. In the end,

Breaux pulled into the case Sgts. Eddie McDonald, John Dean, and Chuck Alford, and each was instructed to meet Ownby and Tyler at Larry's Antique Mall as soon as possible.

The mall now was vacant except for vendors waiting for information on Falyssa. It was dusk but still hot and humid, a remnant of the afternoon rain that now brought out droves of mosquitoes. One of the vendors, a minister, held a prayer vigil before everyone moved inside the main building. They prayed for Falyssa's return and for strength. Because in this darkest hour, there was no place else to turn.

As darkness settled in, detectives began to arrive at the antique mall. Mr. Lavergne, his wife, and their son and his girlfriend had just arrived from Lake Charles and found Elaine and Joe. Michael Van Winkle had also gotten word about his daughter and arrived about the same time.

The burden of first disclosure fell to Lt. Ownby. She ushered family members away from the rest of the crowd. Elaine suddenly realized she was about to hear the most dreaded words a parent can ever hear. Ownby told the family members that from the age, size, and clothing description, the girl found dead in Newton County could be Falyssa. She said that the body had been taken to a funeral home in Kirbyville. Someone needed to go identify her.

Elaine wanted to go but Ownby did not think it was a good idea. Elaine's father volunteered to go with Sgt. Jordan to view the body. Rev. Parks Walker joined them to lend emotional support.

The one-hour drive north from Larry's to Stringer Funeral Home in Kirbyville seemed to last only minutes for Falyssa's grandfather. Once there, the three men from Beaumont met Sheriff Powell, Deputy Whittaker, and Ranger McBride. They entered the mortician's room where the small lifeless form lay on a table covered, except for the face, with a white sheet. The child's hair was still wet and mud-caked. Mud also covered her once pretty face, now badly bloated.

Mr. Lavergne looked closely at the lifeless little body. There was no mistaking -- it was Falyssa.

Mr. Lavergne wanted to leave immediately to be with his daughter and family. A few minutes later he and Rev. Walker left the funeral home and headed to Beaumont. The journey that had seemed so brief now seemed to take forever. Falyssa's grandfather was consumed with one thought: who could be so inhumane?

At 7:30 p.m., the owner of the Mauriceville Flea Market called Larry's with Rex Powell's phone number. Justine called, and a man answered. He said he was Rex Powell. Justine handed the phone to Joe. Joe told Rex that Falyssa had been missing since that morning shortly after Rex had been at their booth. Had he seen anything before he left Larry's that morning? Rex said no, then asked if Joe remembered his coming back to the Langley's booth as he was leaving. Rex reminded him he had told them good-bye and that he would see them in November at the next Old Time Trade Days weekend. Joe replied that he remembered the encounter, but that now, they were grasping at straws trying to find Falyssa. Rex reiterated he had not seen anything and told Joe to call back if he needed anything more.

Back at Larry's Antique Mall, Lt. Tyler took a call from Sgt. Jordan in Kirbyville. Jordan told Tyler that Elaine's father had identified Falyssa. Tyler advised Jordan to stay with the body until identification officers and other detectives could get to the funeral home. Tyler then passed the news on to Lt. Ownby. Again, the task of bearing bad news fell to her. She ushered family members away from the lingering but concerned crowd that remained at Larry's. She told them that the little girl found under the bridge was indeed Falyssa. This news, even though final, was almost anti-climatic for Elaine, because she had braced herself for the worst. Through the shock of it all, whatever her little girl had had to endure, Elaine knew that Falyssa was not being hurt any more. Falyssa was at peace.

There was nothing more the family could do at Larry's. Joe and Elaine were totally drained, and left for the police station with Sgt. Alford. Officers took a short statement from Joe to tie down a few basic details of the day's events. A detailed statement would come later. After the officer finished the statement and signed it, the Langley family headed home to Lake Charles. They were shocked, stunned, and without their little girl. Their lives would never be the same.

Most of the men and women left behind, the investigators, were parents. Each could not help thinking of his or her own children or grandchildren. Sometimes it's easy to forget that men and women who wear a gun and badge are also dads, moms, and grandparents. Human. Each keeping just enough personal emotion intact to drive forward, yet not so much as to cloud objectivity, experience, and professionalism and to rise to the most difficult occasion.

At the funeral home, Eddie McDonald and John Dean met with Bill Jordan and Officer Mike Jones, the Beaumont Police Department's identifications officer on duty. Jones had worked on the streets for several years and was a veteran patrol officer. But he was new to identification, so he called experienced identifications officer Boyd Lamb.

Mike took numerous photos of the body as the officers conducted a visual inspection. A photo is supposed to be worth a thousand words. Mike's photos would leave one almost speechless.

Investigators wrote that Falyssa was fully clothed in a pink shirt and shorts, matching the description given on the Missing Persons report. Falyssa's hands had been tied in front of her with a sash cord and a piece of the same cord tied around her neck pulled so tight that it cut into her skin. Investigators also documented bruising on each leg in the ankle area, which they believed to be caused by her being tied there also.

Additional observations described a discoloration to the face and hands from the lack of circulation, leading one officer to believe Falyssa had been strangled.

A third investigator noted Falyssa's hands were bound in a way resembling livestock.

It was almost midnight when Sheriff Powell suggested the officers return to the crime scene. He wanted, as much as possible, to provide Beaumont investigators with every bit of information and evidence available. As soon as they arrived at Cow Creek Bridge, Boyd Lamb and Mike Jones encircled the crime scene area with yellow tape. They examined by flashlight the mud puddle where Falyssa had been found, the bush where the extra rope had been found, the fresh tire prints and the foot prints that might or might not be connected with the crime. Jones and Lamb were steadily taking photographs, but it was impossible to do an adequate job in the darkness. It was after midnight. Darkness, fatigue, and exasperation finally won. The officers left the bridge and went their separate ways. They'd get a few hours rest and start again. Sunday would be another day.

Newton County Sheriff Wayne Powell

Spring, 1983. Three-year-old Falyssa with Shonna.

CHAPTER SIX

THE INVESTIGATION IN FULL SWING

None of the agencies involved in the investigation had a county morgue or a full-time coroner. The law enforcement agencies in Jefferson County utilized the services of local pathologist, Dr. Thomas Molina.

Contacted late Saturday night, Dr. Molina had requested that Falyssa's body be transported to Broussard's Funeral Home in Beaumont in preparation for the autopsy on Sunday morning.

Sue Kelly, one of Beaumont Police Department's veteran civilian identification technicians, went to Broussard's to view the autopsy. Kelly later wrote in her investigative report that Dr. Molina had her take pictures of Falyssa's body after her clothing had been removed, including photos of the vaginal area. She also photographed the ropes around Falyssa's neck and wrists, and the same areas after the ropes were removed. The ropes were turned over to Kelly as evidence.

Dr. Molina also turned over four vials of blood, and hair samples from Falyssa's head and pubic area, as well as some found on her clothing.

Finally, Dr. Molina completed the rape kit and swabbed a white substance on her left leg. Sue Kelly photographed the white substance and took possession of the rape kit and swabs from Falyssa's leg and throat. Dr. Molina found a piece of plastic in Falyssa's hands, which was turned over as evidence.

Dr. Molina found a secretion coming from the vagina and observed that Falyssa did not have an intact hymen. He found asphyxiation as the cause of death, noting that the knots were expertly tied.

Late Sunday afternoon, Falyssa's body was released to her mother and was transported to Johnson Funeral Home in Lake Charles,

Louisiana.

Chuck Alford met Larry Tinkle at 6:30 a.m. Sunday in Bunnye's Snack Shop in the antique mall. Alford, a twenty-five-year veteran police officer and homicide investigator, knew the best place to find witnesses and clues was at the last place anyone had seen Falyssa. He started at the peanut stand and worked his way through the maze of more than 250 vendors. A physically massive man, Alford had an even bigger task ahead. From the peanut stand, Alford went to Florine Lackey's stand and spoke with Edna Mastus of Montgomery, Texas. Mrs. Mastus said that about the time the little girl came up missing she saw an old brown car pull around the shopping area. Mastus also said that she had been told that a car had hit a child, put it into the car and driven off. She also observed two Hispanic males come out of the woods near the Langley's tent.

Kenneth R. Young, of Brookshire, Texas, was selling guns at Trade Days, and he recalled two Hispanic males did come out of the woods behind him and tried to buy a gun from him.

Security Officer Harry Brown had not seen Falyssa on Saturday but did know her on sight. Darrell Brown, another guard, said he knew Falyssa but had not seen her on Saturday.

Liz Sandell, a high school drill team sponsor said that while she and one of the girls were volunteering parking cars at the entrance, a white man in a brown or maroon panel van became upset when he was not allowed to leave through the gate.

Beaumont's police department is large enough to support specialized units yet still small enough for everyone to know each other, and for the citizens to know the officers. For this case, the Detective Division was divided into two sections under the supervision of Deputy Chief David Ivey.

The main investigative unit consists of officers in the Detective Division under the direction of Captain Gary Breaux. The second investigative unit in the Special Crimes Bureau, which includes the Special Tactics and Response unit and the Youth Services Bureau.

Lt. Frank Coffin, a twenty-year veteran with a bachelor's degree in psychology and a master's degree in police administration, led the Sex Crimes Unit. He had been a detective in the Sex Crimes Unit for ten-years prior to his promotion to lieutenant. His position had been filled by Sgt. Bill Davis. Davis and Coffin began their careers with the Beaumont Police Department on the same day in 1972. Davis specialized in child abuse investigations, both physical and sexual, as well as adult sex crime cases.

Before the Special Crimes Unit was formed, all cases involving a child were assigned to investigators in the Juvenile Division. Davis had been assigned there for several years, investigating almost every reported child abuse case in Beaumont. While Davis investigated child sex crimes, Coffin handled adult sex crimes. Both developed specialized knowledge of dealing with these special types of crimes and the kinds of perpetrators who commit them.

Reports of the tragedy had been on the local news at 10:00 p.m. Saturday night. Sunday morning the *Beaumont Enterprise* headlined Falyssa's article, "Girl 11, abducted in Beaumont, found dead in Newton County." As Coffin read his Sunday morning paper, he picked up the phone and called Captain Gary Breaux. The two men knew without so many words being spoken, that unknown-perpetrator cases like this one can only be solved with an organized cooperative effort.

Coffin arrived at Larry's shortly before 9:00 a.m. Sunday. He met with Detectives Alford and Skinner who were interviewing vendors. Then he called Broussard's Funeral Home to discover that preliminary indications showed that Falyssa had been sexually assaulted.

Coffin was not surprised. Now the motive for Falyssa's kidnapping and subsequent murder was coming to light. Coffin knew that if the results of the autopsy *did* indicate she had been sexually assaulted, the investigators would have a motive. For now, Coffin needed to get a specialist involved to deal with the motive.

Davis was enjoying his morning coffee when the phone rang. Coffin briefed Davis on the case and the autopsy, which was still in progress. As soon as the autopsy was concluded and the sexual assault confirmed, Coffin would call back.

Moments later, Coffin received word that Dr. Molina had finished the autopsy. Falyssa had been raped. Dr. Molina had found what he believed to be semen in her vagina. He had also found more of what he believed to be semen on one of her legs. Tests would have to be conducted at the Jefferson County Regional Crime Lab to be conclusive, but the doctor was confident of his findings. Then Molina announced another interesting discovery. After cutting the cord from Falyssa's neck, Dr. Molina observed the bruising was not severe. The lack of severe bruising, compared with the tightness of the rope when the body was discovered, indicated that the rope had not been nearly as tight around Falyssa's neck at the time of death as it was when her body was found.

Kidnapping coupled with murder automatically made this crime a capital murder. Falyssa's rape made the capital offense even more significant. At 11:00 a.m., Coffin told Davis of the autopsy findings and asked him to come to Larry's as soon as possible.

The investigators were at Bunnye's Snack Shop trying to decide what their next move should be. They discussed Justine Tinkle's call to Rex Powell and about Joe Langley talking to him. Someone still needed to talk with the "Mayor of Mauriceville" to see what he knew.

McBride and the sheriff wanted the Beaumont investigators to see the videotape of the crime scene so they could cover all bases but not duplicate the efforts of others. Tyler and Coffin decided that the case also needed the expertise of Sgt. Bill Tatum, the Supervisor of the Beaumont Police Department's Identification Bureau. He was considered one of the best identification technicians, crime scene experts, and all-round meticulous investigators to be found in the area. Coffin called Tatum but he was playing golf. Coffin left word at the clubhouse for Tatum to call right away. Leaving Larry's, there was just enough time for everyone to grab some fast food and get to the police department's staff conference room for their meeting.

As McBride showed the videotape of the crime scene, the Beaumont investigators saw the body of Falyssa face down in the partially filled mud puddle. They saw tire tracks and the extra rope in a bush close by. A girl's headband was also found near the bush with the extra rope. The officers saw an indention in the mud about five feet from Falyssa's left foot. The officers felt that this may have been where Falyssa's body had initially hit the soft wet dirt before falling forward to its final location. Except for the toes of her shoes, which were in the mud, the shoes were clean. It was apparent Falyssa had not walked around in the mud underneath the bridge. Fresh tire prints close to the body appeared to have been made with a mud-grip tire. The back of Falyssa's right arm from the shoulder to about the middle of the forearm was visible but her hand was under her body. Her face was turned to the right, resting slightly on the left cheek.

As the videotape continued, one of the investigators pointed out shoe prints in the sandy area under the bridge between the body and the creek. The first print was from a cowboy boot. The next two were small with a smooth sole. It seemed possible these were Falyssa's prints. Two more shoe prints that had work-boot type soles were visible and these prints could have been made as the murderer followed Falyssa to the creek. Two more pointed-toed boot prints were seen approaching the creek in the same area, along with an empty Kool filter king cigarette box and an empty Colt 45 malt liquor bottle. The tape stopped, then began again as two officers were turning Falyssa's body onto its left side to see her face. The camera then scanned from the head down to the hands. Usually, when a person has their hands tied or handcuffed in front, the palms are turned inward. As had been previously described and now clearly shown on film, Falyssa's hands were turned toward each other with the palms pointed outward. The rope knot was between the wrists, an uncommon way to tie someone's hands. As the officers focused on what this could mean, the tape ended.

The Beaumont detectives had a bevy of questions about photographs and measurements at the crime scene. Tyler and Coffin decided more exact measurements, photos, and videotaping were needed. About this time, Tatum arrived. After he watched the video with the others, Davis and Tatum left for Newton County. The other detectives were to continue checking out leads in the Beaumont area.

The phone had been ringing off the wall. The news media wanted more information and photos of Falyssa. The two supervisors sent Chuck Alford to Lake Charles to get a recent photo of Falyssa from her family. Other calls had come in from people at Larry's Antique Mall who had not been interviewed and who thought they might have information relating to the case. The investigators also reminded the group that the "Mayor of Mauriceville" had not been interviewed. John Dean was given the assignment of contacting the "Mayor" and getting a statement from him. Coffin and Tyler stayed at the police station to coordinate the detectives' activities, answer phones, and supervise leads and information from Davis, Tatum, and the Newton County investigators.

As the meeting was adjourning and the detectives were heading in their separate directions, Jordan took a call from Sheriff Powell. A white male named Joe Simon*[1] had been arrested by Jasper Police for outstanding traffic violations. At the time of Simon's arrest, some nylon rope had been found in the bed of his pickup truck. He told the arresting officers that he had been in the Beaumont area the day before visiting some relatives. Jordan told the sheriff that he would pass on the

---

[1]   Throughout the book, each * asterisk denotes a fictitious name.

information to Davis and Tatum, who were heading to Cow Creek Bridge. Detective Jordan found Davis preparing to leave and instructed him to go by the Jasper Jail and interview Simon. Jordan agreed to go and talk to Simon's relatives in Beaumont.

Davis and Tatum gassed up their vehicles and headed north on Hwy. 96. It was another clear but unseasonably hot October Sunday afternoon. Driving through the piney woods of East Texas, it felt more like August than October. But this wasn't a leisurely Sunday drive for the two detectives as they sped through heavier-than-normal traffic. Davis and Tatum were thinking the same thing in their separate vehicles. Almost twenty-four hours had passed since Falyssa's body had been discovered, and no significant leads had been uncovered. Both knew that, as a rule, time was not on their side. The more time that passed, the lesser their chances would be to solve this brutal crime, and the greater the chances would be for the murderer to get away with it.

Davis and Tatum were almost out of radio range when the dispatcher's voice cracked across the speaker, followed by Coffin's voice. Sheriff Powell had just reported that a Kirbyville police Officer had stopped two men who might be suspects in the case. Kirbyville is about eight miles west of Cow Creek Bridge. Instead of heading to the Cow Creek Bridge, Davis and Tatum headed to the Kirbyville Police Station.

Jordan left the station and went to visit Simon's relatives. Simon had told Jasper police officers he had visited his aunt and uncle in Beaumont on Saturday; but his relatives told Jordan they had not seen Simon in about two months. They also said that Simon was always getting into trouble with the law. Jordan thanked them for their time and left. Why had Simon lied to the Jasper officers? Jordan relayed to Davis the information he'd received from Simon's relatives. It was information Davis would need to know before he interviewed Simon.

Meanwhile, Alford had made it to Lake Charles. He called Joe and Elaine's house but there was no answer; they were probably at the funeral home. He got directions and drove to Johnson's Funeral Home. The Langleys were not there but the funeral director helped Alford get in touch with the Van Winkles. Alford talked with Mike and his wife, Julie, and they gave him a school photo of Falyssa.

Mike asked if anyone had been arrested. Alford assured them that several detectives were working on the case. There wasn't anything to say except to assure them that all leads were being investigated and everything possible was being done. His answer was honest and sincere, and they knew it. With photo in hand, Alford thanked them and headed back to Beaumont.

At headquarters, John Dean was checking to see if the "Mayor of Mauriceville," Rex Powell, had a local police record. He put a call in to the Orange County Sheriff's Department. Captain Linnes Hubbard, supervisor of the department's Criminal Investigations Division, had heard about the case Saturday afternoon. Dean asked about a man residing in Orange County named Rex Powell who called himself the "Mayor of Mauriceville." Hubbard knew a lot of people in the county, but he didn't know anyone by the name of Rex Powell. He told Dean he'd check this guy out as much as he could and call him back.

Davis and Tatum arrived at the Kirbyville Police Department about 3:00 p.m. Sunday. Curtis Whittaker told them the sheriff had received an interesting call Saturday evening revealing that an old model gray truck had been seen in the area of Cow Creek Bridge shortly before Falyssa's body had been found. Two men in a truck matching that description had been stopped and taken into custody. George Martin* was the driver; Grady Knox* was his passenger. A records check revealed that Knox had been convicted of indecency with a child a few months earlier.

Davis got pertinent information on Knox and then asked his whereabouts the day before. Knox said he had worked all day at a local cattle auction barn. When it was Martin's turn to comment on his whereabouts, he told of being at a house down the road cutting down a tree at the time of the murder. He mentioned that he'd had to wait until the rain stopped to complete the job. Both men were at ease -- not the kind of demeanor normally displayed by someone who had kidnapped, raped, and killed a little girl twenty-four hours earlier. The men were released.

Davis and Tatum met Sheriff Powell for the first time and were impressed by his quick smile. The longer the sheriff talked -- and he loved to talk -- the more the Beaumont officers liked his quick wit and pleasant demeanor. But they knew that if you were a criminal, Wayne Powell could literally become your worst nightmare. As the evening passed, the detectives learned not only about Powell's sincerity and big heart; they sensed that the affable fifty-year-old in typical Texas boots and cowboy hat was a highly effective peace officer who typically "got his man."

Since the two Kirbyville men checked out for now, Powell, Whittaker, Davis, and Tatum drove the eight miles to Cow Creek Bridge, onto the grassy shoulder on the east side of the road. They walked down the steep embankment to the underside of the bridge. Past several pairs of support columns, water flowed along the far west side of the creek bed. Powell and Whittaker pointed out the muddy area where Falyssa's body had been found. They showed the Beaumont officers the suspicious tire tracks and shoe prints, the bush where the extra rope had been discarded, and the location of the headband just past the bush. They walked from the sandy area down a short but steep embankment to the creek itself, trying to find anything that may have been missed.

Did the murderer walk Falyssa down to the creek and then back up the embankment to where she was killed? Was she killed trying to escape? Was she caught and dragged back to the mud hole and then killed? The men spread out, walking up and down the eastern bank. They found a few prints but nothing matching the ones in the sand.

Davis and Tatum climbed back up the embankment. Tatum got his video camera and 35mm camera and Davis got his notepad and tape measure. They had a lot of work to do, and the weather didn't make it any easier. It was a sweltering afternoon and there wasn't a puff of breeze underneath the bridge.

Davis realized that one map of measurements would not suffice. He decided to make three. The first included measurements of Hwy. 1416, from Hwy. 87 to the bridge. The second showed the eastern side of the bridge to the creek. Davis observed that to get under the bridge, a person could drive from the western side of the bridge, down either the north road or the south road from the highway. But to get back to the highway, the south road was the only feasible way. The large mud hole, the steepness of the embankment, and the pot holes in the asphalt on the north side embankment made it impossible to go up on that side.

The investigators began to theorize that the murderer, with Falyssa in the vehicle, drove at a high rate of speed down the north embankment and through the large mud hole, splashing mud and water everywhere. He stopped under the bridge long enough for mud and water to drip from the bumper and undercarriage, then dumped Falyssa's body, drove out from under the bridge along the south road and climbed the embankment back to the highway. The driver had to have been going fast to make it up the steep embankment. Wayne pointed out more mud drippings past the hole just under the south side of the bridge. These made it seem that the vehicle had stopped under the bridge a second time.

Davis's third drawing showed the immediate crime scene. He included the measurements of the mud hole where Falyssa had been found, the tire tracks, and the small shoe prints. If the crime scene needed to be re-created for a judge and jury, the maps, photos, and video would make the task possible.

While Davis mapped and measured, Tatum was busy gathering samples. With a pocket full of plastic evidence bags, he began with the asphalt on the embankment of the northern road. There were some fresh gouge marks that could have been caused by the murderer's fast-moving vehicle.

Tatum and Davis looked over the scene. They had videoed, photographed, and measured everything they could think of. At times they had been on their hands and knees scouring the area for evidence. Had they missed anything? They had been at the bridge, mainly under   it, for more than three hours. As they climbed the embankment they felt they had done as thorough a job as possible.

Falyssa and Shonna's mother often had the girls'
photographs taken twice a year - once in spring or
summer and again at Christmas. Here, in 1983,
the girls show off their new bathing suits.

CHAPTER SEVEN

A COMING TOGETHER

Local criminal records showed nothing on Rex Powell. Even more curious, there was no Rex Powell listed in the phone book. Detective Dean dialed the number he'd been given earlier. Rex Powell answered the phone.

Dean introduced himself and told Rex his reason for calling. When Dean asked Rex if he would come to the station for a statement, the man became defensive. He wanted to know why he had to give a statement. He had already told the people at Larry's Antique Mall and the little girl's step-dad all that he knew, he told Dean. The detective was surprised by Rex's sudden change in attitude. Dean explained to Rex that he was not suspected of anything and that the police just wanted a sworn statement detailing the locations and times he had seen Falyssa on Saturday morning. When Dean asked Rex for his address, the witness again became adamant about not wanting to get involved. Dean again asked for the address, and finally Rex said, "405 Lazy Lane, Mauriceville."

When Dean asked Rex for his date of birth, the witness recoiled again. Why did Dean need his date of birth? What did that have to do with his having seen the little girl for a few minutes? Keeping cool, Dean explained to Rex that his name, address, and date of birth were all part of a routine investigation. But Rex refused, telling Dean he'd come in Monday and give his statement. Then he abruptly hung up. Dean sat there for a minute while his investigative senses kicked into high gear. Something wasn't right. A phone call that should have been very simple suddenly wasn't.

Coffin was in the conference room with Robert Hobbs, ace investigator from District Attorney Tom Maness' office, when Detective Dean returned with news of his troublesome conversation with Rex. They decided to check further into Rex's background, and not wait until Monday to get a statement. Dean went back to his office and called Rex. When Dean told the witness that his statement could not wait until Monday, Rex complained that he had no means of transportation. Dean told the witness that he and another detective would come get him then take him back home. The detective knew he had put Rex Powell between a rock and a hard place. If Rex refused, it would cause further suspicion. Rex agreed to be ready when the detectives arrived.

Captain Hubbard called Sgt. Vernon Odom, who was patrolling in Mauriceville, and asked the deputy to drive by 405 Lazy Lane, check on the address, get a description of the residence, and see if any vehicles were there.

Sgt. Odom found that the residence was a mobile home. Parked next to the trailer was a motor home. Odom checked the license plate. It was registered to Rex Powell at a post office box in Bon Wier, Texas, located between Newton and the Louisiana state line.

With this information, Captain Hubbard's next call was to the Texas Department of Public Safety. He requested a driver's license check on all "R. Powell's." It wasn't long before the dispatcher called back. She had what he wanted -- a James Rexford Powell, white male, 405 Lazy Lane, date of birth August 23, 1946, and a driver's license number. Hubbard entered Powell's statistics into the state and national criminal database. In a few seconds the computer began to print out its findings -- Rex had been arrested on prior occasions in DeRidder, Louisiana, for aggravated rape, attempted aggravated murder, and aggravated burglary. James "Rex" Rexford Powell was definitely proving interesting. He might not be the killer, but he was definitely worth further investigation.

Coffin and Hubbard placed calls to the Beauregard Parish, Louisiana Sheriff's Department and talked with Deputy Detective Robert McCullough, who, it turns out, was quite familiar with Rex Powell. McCollough had investigated several cases with Rex as a suspect. One involved an attack on an elderly woman. In an attempted sexual assault, the elderly victim fought back, and her attacker shot her in the left ear. She had identified Rex, there had been a trial and Rex had been found not guilty.

Rex had also been suspected in a couple of arsons, and in the sexual assault of a twelve-year-old girl. There had not been enough evidence to file any charges against him in the fires or the child's rape. McCollough was the first to recognize that Rex Powell was quickly turning from just another witness into a prime suspect.

During the day, several Newton County residents had called the sheriff's department with information they hoped might help solve Falyssa's murder. One was from Mary Jenkins of Bon Wier. She said on Saturday afternoon a white man driving a large cargo van had driven down her dead-end road. He appeared to be lost. She said the van was white in color, but very dirty, with a big red bird painted on each side. She said the man turned around at the end of her road and then left.

Hearing this, Captain Hubbard radioed Sgt. Odom and asked him to describe Rex's motor home. The sergeant radioed back that the motor home was white in color, with a big red bird painted on each side near the rear of the vehicle.

Rex had been at Larry's just before Falyssa's disappearance. Now, his motor home had possibly been spotted a short distance from the Cow Creek Bridge within an hour of the discovery of Falyssa's body. Suddenly, leads eighty miles apart were developing about the same man at the same time. The investigators could feel it: a sudden coming together of leads. Coffin sent officers to Mauriceville. It was time to pay a visit to Mr. James Rexford Powell.

Silver-capped baby teeth might have kept other children from smiling for
the camera, but not Falyssa. Of several poses taken in the summer
of 1985, she liked this one best.

CHAPTER EIGHT

A NIGHT OF RECKONING

Darkness had settled as Detectives Dean and Jordan met Captain Hubbard in Mauriceville. Hubbard led the way to 405 Lazy Lane. Some distance away, Sgt. Odom maintained surveillance of Powell's residence.

The three men approached the mobile home and knocked on the door. A moment later a man answered. The officers identified themselves, and asked to speak to Rex Powell. "I'm Rex," said the short, medium-built man. He needed a shave. His hair hadn't seen a comb in a while. He wore glasses and a plaid, western-style, long-sleeve shirt, blue jeans, and tennis shoes.

Jordan and Dean asked Rex if he would like to follow them to Beaumont in his motor home. He said he'd rather ride with them. Rex locked his trailer and left with the two Beaumont detectives.

Rex rode in the back seat for the thirty-minute drive from Mauriceville to Beaumont. The detectives did not want to start talking with Rex until they had reached the police station. Rex broke the silence. He told how he had been injured on an oil rig about a year and a half earlier. He told them of the injury to his back and how he now walked at times with a limp. He told them how the injury had left him impotent. He told Dean and Jordan that he and his wife had not had sex in the last year and a half because of his impotence. The two detectives thought it was strange that this man was suddenly discussing his sex life. Was Rex trying to tell them something?

The news media had only reported Falyssa's kidnapping and murder. The sexual assault had not been discovered until earlier that day, and so had not been publicized. The only ones who knew about Falyssa's rape were Dr. Milona, law enforcement personnel involved in the investigation, and, of course, the murderer. Was Rex trying to build an alibi by telling the detectives he couldn't have sex?

While Rex traveled to Beaumont, Davis and Tatum were busy in Newton County. They went to Mary Jenkin's home, along with Sheriff Powell and Curtis Whittaker. The middle-aged black woman, with a simple and honest face, immediately recognized Whittaker and Powell and greeted them. Powell asked her about the vehicle she had seen on her street.

"It was about 1:00 p.m., or so, on Saturday," Mrs. Jenkins said. "It had rained and I had finished some housework. I went to sit on the front porch where it was cooler. I had been sitting there for a few minutes when I heard a truck coming down the road," she said. "I thought the mail truck was coming because this truck sounded just like it. But it was this white cargo type van," she explained.

The driver was a white man with long dark blonde or brown hair. He drove into a driveway at the end of her dead-end road and sat there, revving the engine. Mrs. Jenkins said he just sat there for a few minutes, "like he didn't know where he was going." He then backed the big vehicle up, and drove down the dirt road back to the highway.

What Mrs. Jenkins said next stunned the officers. She said the word around town was that this vehicle almost ran three young men off the road the day before by Cow Creek Bridge. She asked Powell if he knew a young black man named Elmer and described to him where Elmer lived.

If this information was true, and the officers had no reason to believe it wasn't, they now had information that Rex had not only been seen in the vicinity of the bridge by Mrs. Jenkins' house, he might have been at Cow Creek Bridge, only a few feet from where Falyssa's body had been discovered.

At about the same time Mrs. Jenkins was dropping her bombshell, Rex arrived at the Beaumont Police Station. He was escorted to Jordan's office. Dean came in to ask if he could look at the bottoms of Rex's tennis shoes. The shoes were Reeboks with the word

"Reebok" molded into the sole. This was important because one of the tennis shoe prints Dean had seen in the sand at the creek had the letters"__ebok."

Dean left the office and Jordan continued the interview. Rex told of his association with Larry's Antique Mall, how he used to set up his motor home on one of the lots at Old Time Trade Days and sell antique tools, jars, and other things. Because of his back injury in 1989 he had to quit. Since that time, he usually went to Old Time Trade Days to visit friends and acquaintances. Jordan asked specifically about the events of Saturday. Rex told him he had left home and driven to Old Time Trade Days after his wife had left for work. He named about half a dozen people he had visited with while walking around the mall grounds.

He said he arrived at Joe Langley's display booth and travel trailer about 8:30 a.m. Rex said he visited with Joe and Falyssa for about fifteen to twenty minutes. He remembered that Falyssa was eating dry cereal and griping because Joe and Elaine had forgotten to bring milk. He then left the Langley's booth but saw Falyssa again by the peanut vendor's stand. He said they briefly spoke to one another. Rex kept walking and Falyssa walked beside him for a short distance, he said. Rex then stopped and visited with an old friend for a few minutes and Falyssa continued past him. He didn't know where she went and he never saw her again.

He told Jordan that he went back to his motor home, unlocked it, got in and left. Jordan wanted to know more. Rex said he headed south on Eastex Freeway and took IH-10 east. He turned onto Texas Hwy. 12 in Vidor, and onto Mesquite Road, taking back roads to his residence. Rex punctuated his statement by saying that the last time he had seen Falyssa was by the peanut stand; he had not taken her away from Larry's or hurt her. Rex continued that the first he had heard that the child had been killed was when Sgt. Dean had called him at his home. Rex then read his written statement, swore it was true and correct to the best of his knowledge, and signed the document.

Jordan's questions had been very exact. His investigative experience had prompted definite answers. If the investigation warranted a request that Rex voluntarily submit to a polygraph examination he could not elaborate because of the structure and simplicity of his initial statements in his affadivat. His answers would have to be a simple "Yes" or "No."

As the focus of the investigation narrowed, the detectives were mindful of the legal hurdles in a case like this. They all knew of horrendous cases where the system finds the suspect guilty only to have an appellate court reverse the verdict on a legal technicality. Coffin and Hobbs decided it was time to call Assistant District Attorney Paul McWilliams, who was very experienced in capital crimes.

McWilliams was briefed about the case -- especially about Rex Powell. McWilliams said he'd be at the Beaumont Police Department within minutes.

In Newton County, Davis, Tatum, and Powell set out to find Elmer Hopkins. Driving down a remote gravel-and-dirt road in the dark of night, Sheriff Powell flagged down an oncoming vehicle to ask where Elmer lived. By Divine providence, the passengers were none other than the Hopkins brothers themselves. Tatum, Davis and Powell had caught up with them just in time; they were headed to take Elmer to Corpus Christi to his post at the naval base there.

Elmer and Albert Hopkins excitedly told the sheriff and investigators about their encounter with a speeding motor home Saturday afternoon near Cow Creek Bridge. It was about 2:30 p.m., give or take a few minutes when it happened, the men said. As they turned off Hwy. 87 onto Hwy. 1416 and crossed Cow Creek Bridge, a white motor home came flying up the right side of the embankment and turned right on the paved highway in front of them. Both men said the motor home had come from the dirt road that runs alongside the paved road and goes back under Cow Creek Bridge. Elmer said he'd had to swerve quickly into the oncoming lane to keep from colliding with the big vehicle. Albert said the first thing he saw was a big red eagle on the motor home. As Elmer swerved into the other lane, he slammed on the accelerator and went on around the motor home. As they passed it, Albert and Elmer both said they noticed the driver, a white male.

After the two men finished their stories the lawmen were almost certain they had their killer.

Back in Beaumont, Coffin listened intently as Bill Davis told him of the brothers' story. Coffin told Davis that Rex was just completing a written statement. Their timing couldn't have been better. Their conversation ended with Coffin's usual, "Keep me posted."

Jordan left Rex in the office reading his statement and walked over to the Detective Division's main room. Jordan explained to Coffin that he was unable to get Rex to budge from his original story. But Jordan was not aware of Davis's information from Newton County. Nonetheless, Rex was still a witness, not a suspect, and the investigators continued to treat him as a witness. He had stepped out of Jordan's office several times to smoke a cigarette and had gone to the restroom without escort. He was not under arrest and could have stopped the interview or left the police station at any time. By his actions and words, he let the interview continue of his own free will and accord.

Coffin notarized the sworn statement of James Rexford Powell. Relying upon his investigative and psychological expertise, he asked Rex a hypothetical question: "What would you say if I told you we have a witness who saw you in the area of Cow Creek Bridge in Newton County?"

As Coffin might have expected, Rex changed his story. He said that after he left Larry's Antique Mall he drove home; he just stayed for about two hours. Then he drove to Newton County to A.J. Satterwhite's Country Store.

Satterwhite is a Justice of the Peace in Newton County, and operates his country store on Hwy. 363 between Bon Wier and

Kirbyville. Coffin asked Rex if he visited with Satterwhite and Rex said yes, adding that he was only there for a few minutes. Coffin asked why Rex had made such a long drive to the store for just a minute and then made the lone drive back home. Rex explained that Satterwhite has an antique auction in the back room of his store on Saturday nights. Rex had left some things there some weeks earlier and wanted to see if any of the items had been sold. It was official; Rex had changed his original story, and in so doing had involved a judge in his alibi.

Rex wouldn't change his story again. But Coffin had noticed in Rex some body language that can be indicative of extreme stress and possible deception. The "Mayor of Mauriceville" had become nervous, tapping his feet, making his legs jump, and crossing his arms and legs after Coffin asked a question. But Rex stuck to his story after his authorized changes were made to the affidavit.

Coffin thanked Rex for his cooperation. Jordan took Rex home. Later the detective would learn that as he and Rex headed toward Mauriceville, a three-car caravan passed them, bound for Beaumont with what promised to be startling new evidence in the death of Falyssa Van Winkle.

The caravan arrived at the Beaumont Police Department and everyone went upstairs to the Detective Division, which resembled an ant hill at that moment. Davis escorted Albert Hopkins to his office to take his statement. McWilliams considered all the known facts about Rex. He was sure there was probable cause for a search and arrest warrant. Others got busy preparing a search and arrest warrant affidavit on a laptop computer.

At the same time, things were heating up in Mauriceville. At 11:30 p.m. Orange County Deputies Jerry Hussey and Craig King relieved Sgt. Odom of his surveillance position across the street from Rex Powell's house. They'd been at their position just a few minutes when they noticed a man and a woman come out of the mobile home, walk to the station wagon, and load suitcases into it. A couple of minutes later, Hussey and King radioed to Hubbard that the woman was leaving the residence in the station wagon and the man was returning to the mobile home.

Detective Jordan was oblivious to this as he drove back to Beaumont. It had been a long day; he was exhausted. He was scheduled to take two days vacation on Monday and Tuesday. With the day's events swimming in his head, Jordan almost didn't hear the police dispatcher call him. Coffin's voice came over the radio. He wanted Jordan to stop right away and call him from a pay phone. Jordan stopped at a convenience store just east of the intersection of Hwy. 12 and Hwy. 62. Coincidentally, Sheriff Powell was also there using the phone. Coffin told Jordan of the soon-to-be-completed search and arrest warrant and asked him to return to Rex's house and maintain surveillance. Jordan reminded Coffin of his days off and Coffin promised he'd send John Dean immediately to relieve him.

Jordan saw that Sheriff Powell had also finished his conversation on another pay phone. He told the sheriff what was in the works in Beaumont. While they were talking, they overheard Sgt. Hussey and Capt. Hubbard on the police radio discussing the activity at Rex Powell's trailer. It looked like business was about to pick up.

Jordan jumped in his vehicle and headed toward Rex's house. Shortly after turning off Hwy. 62, he met a light blue Subaru station wagon traveling in the opposite direction. He recognized the vehicle and it was driven by a white female. But his assignment was not to stop the station wagon. It was to set up surveillance on the motor home, so he continued toward Rex Powell's house.

The light blue Subaru drove out of the subdivision onto Hwy. 62 towards Hwy. 12, straight toward the group of lawmen who were still at the intersection. It headed east onto Hwy. 12. Seconds later, Orange County Deputy Sherry Goodwin, who was with the lawmen at the intersection, pursued the Subaru and stopped it without incident.

Goodwin approached and shined her flashlight inside the car. She noticed the suitcase in the backseat. She asked the woman for her driver's license. It identified her as Coliss Lynn Powell. Deputy Goodwin asked her if she was Rex Powell's wife. Corliss said yes, and that seemed to be all it took for her to come clean with what she and her husband were up to.

Corliss said she and Rex knew that officers were going to search the motor home, so she didn't want to be there. She had packed a suitcase and was on her way to her parents' house in Merryville, Louisiana. Deputy Goodwin asked if she could look in the suitcase. Hesitantly, Corliss gave her permission. Goodwin filled out a Consent to Search Form and Corliss signed it. In the suitcase was not one piece of women's clothing -- only men's clothing. Corliss admitted that she and Rex had planned for her to leave the house and then he would sneak out the back of the mobile home and travel on foot through the wooded area behind their home to a back road, where she would pick him up later that night.

Several times during her conversation, Corliss Powell said she didn't want to say anything that might incriminate her husband. When Goodwin asked Corliss where she had been on Saturday, Mrs. Rex Powell replied that she had worked from 7 a.m. to 7 p.m., and could not verify her husband's whereabouts during that time. When she got home Rex told her that the father of the little girl who had been kidnapped from Larry's Antique Mall had called. Rex told Corliss he'd seen the girl and her family while visiting Larry's that morning, but that was all he knew. She said Rex knew the dead girl and her family, but that she had never met them.

Satisfied for the moment, Goodwin allowed Corliss to leave. She drove away, continuing east towards Louisiana.

Coffin listened intently as Sheriff Powell phoned to say that Corliss had been stopped, the suitcase contained men's clothing, and the couple had planned to escape to avoid possible apprehension. The sheriff passed this news on to McWilliams and Hobbs.

In McWilliam's prosecutorial thinking, the affidavit requesting the search and arrest warrant appeared to have sufficient probable cause.

Part One described the motor home. Part Two described evidentiary items constituting capital murder. These included rope, blood, semen, soil samples, clothing, fibers, hair, peanuts, and fingerprints. Part Three named the person in charge of the suspected place and premises: James Rexford Powell. Part Four stated that the person who would swear these facts were true and correct to the best of his knowledge, Lt. Frank Coffin, believed Rex had committed capital murder and was concealing property and items constituting evidence. Part Five consisted of a brief synopsis of the case. Finally, the affidavit requested a warrant for the arrest of James Rexford Powell, recommending that hair and blood be taken from Rex by a doctor, registered nurse, or qualified medical technician upon his arrest.

Coffin and his colleagues read and re-read the affidavit. Was it sufficient? Did it contain too little or too much information? Did it show sufficient probable cause? Would it withstand the legal scrutiny of a state district judge, the magistrates of the Texas Criminal Court of Appeals, a federal judge, the 5th Circuit Court of Appeals, and the United States Supreme Court? All agreed that it would. McWilliams, Coffin, and Hobbs were en route to Criminal District Judge Larry Gist's residence with the warrant and affidavit.

Davis and Tatum arrived back at the intersection in Mauriceville and filled in the others about the impending search and arrest warrant. It had been hot all day, and now, in the middle of the night it had not gotten any cooler. The stars were out, but the air was so thick it was hard to breathe. The stress had been constant and would soon rise again. Sheriff Powell lightened the load, if only for a short while, with a joke and a good laugh among his friends. Just as everyone was beginning to wonder if something had happened to the crew from Beaumont, they arrived. Just Gist had issued the warrant. The night of reckoning for James Rexford Powell had begun.

A procession of a dozen or more police cars filled Rex's front yard. The uniformed Orange County deputies ran to the back of Rex's property to prevent escape. Captain Hubbard radioed his dispatcher and had them phone Rex. When the "Mayor of Mauriceville" answered, the dispatcher told him he needed to step outside his mobile home with his hands clearly visible. The dispatcher assured Rex that no one wanted to hurt him. After a long pause, Rex said he'd be out "in a minute."

One minute turned into two, then three. The tension was unbearable. Did Rex have a gun inside? Would he commit suicide? The door finally opened and Rex stepped onto his front porch looking drained but relieved. Captain Hubbard ordered him to put his hands on his head and walk to the front gate. Captain Hubbard frisked him and removed a pocket knife from his jeans pocket. Hobbs advised Rex that he was under arrest for capital murder. His next words cut through the thick night air and brought the investigation closer to its inevitable end.

> *"You have the right to remain silent. If you give up that right, anything you say can and will be used against you in a court of law,"* Hobbs said clearly. *"You have the right to an attorney. If you cannot afford an attorney, one will be appointed for you. And, you have the right to stop questioning at any time you so desire."* Hobbs asked Rex if he understood his rights. Rex replied with a simple *"yes."*

Davis, who had been standing to the side, now stepped behind Rex. He handcuffed first the left wrist, then the right. It would not be the last time that Davis would have the honor of putting handcuffs on the "Mayor of Mauriceville." It was 3:30 a.m., Monday, October 8, forty-one hours after Falyssa Van Winkle had disappeared.

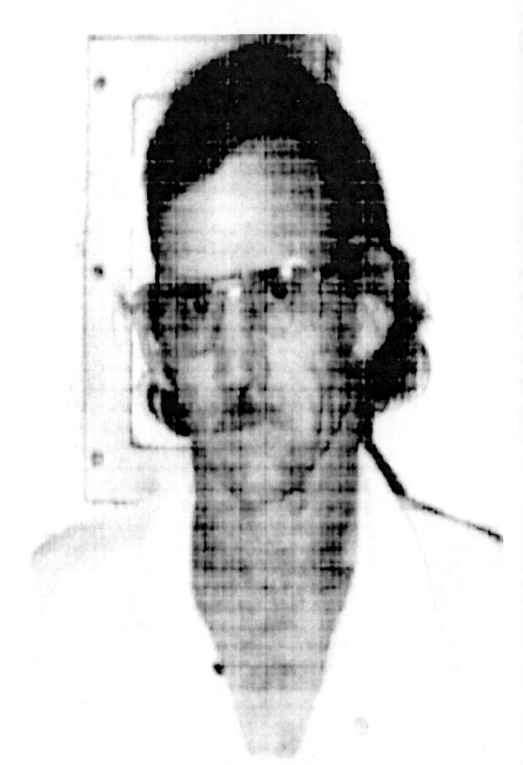

James Rexford Powell after arrest.

Rex Powell's motor home at his residence, photographed moments after his arrest.

CHAPTER NINE

SUNDAY CONTINUES

As Rex watched from the backseat of Davis's detective car, Tatum took photographs of the motor home on the concrete slab in front of the suspect's mobile home. Examining the rear bumper, Tatum noticed some dirt lodged underneath. He collected a sample. It was clear that the motor home looked very clean, like it had been washed within the last few hours. On the concrete about midway on the driver's side was some loose dirt that appeared to have fallen off, or been washed off. Tatum collected a sample of this, too. He looked over the rest of the vehicle and did not see anything that might not survive the tow to the Beaumont Police Department. With Tatum on one side of the motor home and Davis on the other, they placed a tape measure on the outer edge of each rear tire. The width was six feet five inches -- the same measurement as the tracks under Cow Creek Bridge.

Tatum called for a large wrecker. One of the Orange County Deputies went to the nearest intersection and led the wrecker driver to Rex's house.

When an accused person is charged with a crime in one county, arrested in a different county, then is returned to the initial county, Texas law requires that he or she appear before a magistrate to have rights read and bond set before leaving the county they were arrested in. Captain Hubbard advised the Beaumont lawmen that Justice of the Peace Claude Wimberley was the nearest magistrate.

Heading for Wimberley's residence, Captain Hubbard took the back roads as Sheriff Powell had done earlier. Coffin had no idea where they were. Davis mentioned that maybe Rex knew where they were, since he was familiar with the area. He asked, "Hey Rex, do you have any idea where we are?" There was no response. In a louder voice, Davis called again, "Hey Rex!" Still no response from the capital murder suspect in the backseat. Davis turned on the dome light to find

Rex in a semi-reclining position with his head on the top of the back seat. Could Rex have taken an overdose of drugs before leaving his motor home? Did they need to take him to a hospital to try and save him from a suicide attempt? The men watched and listened to Rex, finally realizing he was *sound asleep* -- completely relaxed in the back seat of a police car about to be charged with capital murder. Rex had been nervous and hyperactive earlier at the police station. Once he was arrested, the anxiety was gone. He appeared to be at ease, at least for now.

Captain Hubbard had his dispatcher call to awaken Judge Wimberley a few minutes before they arrived at about 4:00 a.m. Davis woke Rex and helped him out of the car. Davis noticed that Rex was now walking with a limp and needed some assistance. He asked him if something was wrong. Rex told him he'd been the victim of an oil rig accident about a year and a half earlier and had injured his hip. Sitting for a long period of time had caused the old injury to act up. Bill stored this tidbit for future reference as they reached the judge's back door.

Judge Wimberley was sitting at his dining table in pajamas, robe, and slippers. Rex was seated next to the judge at his instruction. Wimberley filled in the name, date, and time on the Arraignment Form. Next, he gave Rex the Miranda and again, Rex agreed that he understood his rights. The judge then asked for a brief synopsis of the crime Rex was alleged to have committed. Hobbs told the judge Rex was accused of kidnapping a ten-year-old girl from Larry's Antique Mall in Beaumont, taking her to Newton County, raping her, and then strangling her to death. Wimberley set Rex's bond at $500,000.

A warrant issued by a magistrate commands an officer to take a person into custody for a specific alleged crime, to be dealt with according to law. The search and arrest warrant issued by Judge Gist was in three parts. The first was the Arrest Warrant. The second enabled the police to take Rex's motor home into custody and search it for any evidence of the kidnapping, sexual assault, or murder. The third part allowed for the collection of specific physical evidence from the suspect himself.

The officers left Judge Wimberley's home and drove to the Emergency Department of Baptist Hospital in Beaumont. While the officers waited for nurses to draw Rex's blood, they started gathering hair samples. Coffin had Rex comb his hair with a comb from a Sexual Assault Examination Kit. The comb was put into an envelope. Coffin then had Rex drop his jeans and underwear. He handed Rex another comb and had the suspect comb his pubic hair. The comb was placed into a third envelope and sealed. Finally, Coffin had Rex pull out several pubic hairs. They were put in the last envelope, and sealed. The hair samples would be sent to the F.B.I. Laboratory in Washington, D.C. for analysis.

A nurse arrived and drew two vials of blood from Rex's arm and handed them to Coffin. These vials of vital evidence would also be analyzed in the due course of the investigation. Coffin left the hospital for headquarters.

Rex had a different destination. Davis and Hobbs took him to the Jefferson County Jail. The huge steel gate topped with strands of razor-sharp barbed wire opened. Davis drove inside the compound. Rex's passage through the gate would end one life and begin another.

Davis had one of the jailers bring him an inmate uniform and two large plastic garbage bags. He and Rex entered the holding cell and walked to the bathroom area. Davis cut open one side and the bottom of one of the plastic bags. He placed it on the floor and had Rex stand on it to remove his shoes and socks. Next, Rex removed his jeans, shirt, t-shirt, and underwear. The clothes were placed in a pile beside the shoes. These clothes would be turned over to Tatum, and, ultimately, sent to Jefferson County Crime Lab to be checked for foreign matter such as hair or blood. Davis folded the opened plastic bag along with its contents and carefully placed it into the second plastic bag.

Dawn was breaking across the Neches River. It was early Monday, but for the investigators the events of Sunday were not over yet.

Rex's motor home was parked in the sallyport on the basement level of the police station. Tatum tied crime scene tape around the vehicle so others would know it was an evidentiary vehicle. He looked over all four sides of the vehicle, and from bottom to top, to make sure everything was secured. On the top, he noticed a fresh dent in what appeared to be a homemade, sheet-metal air conditioner cowling. Could the damage have occurred on the underside of the bridge as Rex left the murder scene?

In the Identification Department, officers examined Rex's clothing. Rex's tennis shoes had the word 'Reebok' molded into the sole. One of the shoe prints in the sand under the bridge showed the last four letters of the word 'Reebok.' Despite the hour and their fatigue, Davis and Tatum immediately returned to Cow Creek Bridge.

With Rex's shoe in hand, Tatum descended the embankment and walked to the sandy area. He saw that the shoe print in question had not been disturbed. He put Rex's shoe next to the sandy imprint for comparison. It wasn't even close. The imprint in the sand was much larger. Tatum noticed further that even though both Rex's shoe and the imprint had 'Reebok' on the sole, the designs were different.

Tatum was tired, disgusted, and thinking there were probably thousands of Reebok tennis shoes in the area with the same sole design. But lack of a match didn't mean that Rex had not been under the bridge. It only meant that he wasn't the one who had made *that* imprint in the sand. Rex Powell was the murderer and Tatum knew it. He drove back across Cow Creek Bridge and headed for Beaumont.

Davis was driving between Kirbyville and Hwy. 87 when he spotted Tatum headed in the opposite direction. They stopped to talk, and Tatum told Davis the shoe and the print didn't match. Davis asked Tatum if he'd checked the underside of the bridge for fresh scrape marks. Tatum had forgotten to look. Tatum then asked Davis if he wanted to go back to the bridge. Neither wanted to be the first one to say, "Let's quit." Off they went to Cow Creek Bridge, again.

They scurried down the embankment and walked briskly to the mud hole. They both looked up directly above at the concrete support beams, all of which had the customary dull "gray" appearance caused by normal weathering. All except one. On the next to the last support beam was a fresh scrape, showing fresh light gray concrete under the dull gray of the rest of the beams. The scrape was above and slightly to the left of the point between the tire tracks. The dent on the air conditioner cowling was on the left, which would match.

Davis and Tatum measured the exact location of the scrape. They imagined that when Rex drove through the huge mud hole he was probably afraid he would get stuck so he parked his motor home just under the bridge next to the support. After he had dumped Falyssa's body, he probably shoved the vehicle into gear, accelerated, then heard what sounded like something shearing off the top of the motor home. He stopped to see what had happened, which would explain the second piles of dirt similar to the ones by the mud hole. Davis and Tatum further surmised that after hurriedly checking his vehicle, Rex sped along the south dirt road and floored the accelerator to climb the steep embankment. Davis and Tatum guessed that Rex's eyes must have popped out of his head when he encountered Elmer Hopkins' pickup on the highway at the top of the embankment, indelibly tying his vehicle to the scene.

The investigators went their separate ways for the first time in two days. Davis arrived at the station and went to his office. He called Mary Jenkins to set up an appointment for her to come to the Beaumot Police Department and identify the motor home. She agreed to come at 9:00 a.m. the next day.

For the investigators, much needed rest had come at last; but for the Langleys, the Van Winkles, and the Lavergnes, the horrible reality was just beginning.

Falyssa at six, enjoying the East Texas countryside.

CHAPTER TEN

THE MOTOR HOME

"Killer hanged girl, authorities say," screamed the headline on the *Beaumont Enterprise* Monday morning. The first paragraph read, "A ten-year-old- girl's killer hanged her before dumping her body under a bridge Saturday, authorities said Sunday evening."

The truth was, while at the bridge Saturday one person posed this scenario, but it didn't fit, and that was the end of that theory. Sadly, the rumor spread like wildfire. Investigators had been available to answer questions from the media Saturday afternoon, Sunday, and Sunday night. If they had been asked about the hanging theory, they could have dispelled it immediately.

Boyd Lamb and Sarah Moon, who was a respected civilian identification technician, started processing the motor home for evidence about 11:00 a.m. They took pictures from every angle to show dents, dirty spots and unique features. They photographed the damage to the air conditioner cowling and the width and tread design of the tires.

Moon dusted for latent fingerprints on and around the exterior passenger door handle. Using a smooth, flowing motion with her brush, Moon spread the special powder and revealed the first latent fingerprint. She tore off a piece of tape and placed it gently over the print. She slowly pulled the tape from the metal surface and put it on a 3 x 5 inch card to preserve for later comparison. Spreading the dust over a wider area, Moon found two other prints in the same area. Both were above and to the left of the door handle. Another fingerprint turned up to the right of the handle below the passenger door's window.

Inside the motor home, Moon found more latent prints on the bottom of the left corner of the window, and others at the top of the door facing, about the inside door latch to the right of the lock, and half an inch to the left of the lock. Next, Moon stepped inside the vehicle and surveyed its structure and contents. As she looked around inside the place where a little ten-year-old girl might have been raped and murdered, she thought of her own children, two boys and two girls. She thought of the many times she had taken her children to the same antique mall, thinking nothing of them returning home safely.

Two green coffee mugs sat in two of the four cup holders in the console between the driver's and passenger's seats. Moon found prints on both. In the little bathroom of the motor home, Moon found prints on the mirror and frame of the medicine cabinet.

A few days later Moon compared the unknown prints with the known fingerprints of Rex and Falyssa. When she was finished, she was not able to match any of them. Her hours of painstaking work had failed to produce any evidence linking Falyssa to Rex and his vehicle.

Meanwhile, Boyd Lamb was looking for other evidence that could prove Falyssa's had been in the motor home. He began at the back door of the vehicle on his hands and knees, methodically scanning the plywood floor. Within minutes, he saw it. Jammed under a small splinter of wood in the floor was a long strand of hair. He photographed it, removed it from under the splinter, placed it in a plastic bag, and sealed it for analysis.

Lamb's experience and expertise told him that the most logical way for this hair to wind up under the splinter was for someone's head to have been dragged over the floor.

Lamb also discovered several sections of rope in a drawer near the rear door of the motor home. The rope looked similar to the ropes he's seen around Falyssa's neck and wrists. He collected the section of rope with the ligatures found on Falyssa's body. He found more long strands of hair on the passenger's sofa cushion, on the floor near the center of the aisle, on the floor by the passenger's seat, on the driver's floorboard, and -- strangely -- on the hinge of the driver's vent window.

Though the vehicle looked like it had been cleaned inside and out recently, Lamb did find some dirt and dried mud on the driver's floorboard. He was aware of the soil samples Tatum had taken from under the bridge so he collected these for comparison. While he was collecting the sample, something under the driver's seat caught his eye. It was another piece of rope tied in a loop then cut in two. Lamb knew there had been evidence indicating that Falyssa's ankles had been bound at some point, although they were not bound when she was found. Had Rex forgotten to get rid of this piece of evidence? Was it in fact the missing piece of rope that had been used to bind Falyssa's legs? He tagged this last piece of evidence, then locked the vehicle.

Davis's first task the next day was to measure the height clearance of the motor home and compare it to his measurements at the bridge. Assisted by Sgt. Don Bailey of the Crimes-Against-Persons Unit, Davis got a ten-foot step ladder and headed to the sallyport. He climbed the ladder and stepped onto the roof of the motor home. The air conditioner cowling did in fact appear to have fresh scrape marks across the front. But the most noticeable damage was on the front driver's side of the cowling, which was not only freshly scraped but also slightly buckled.

The weather was starting to get nasty. A cold front was coming in and the sky was turning dark in the northwest. As Davis and Baily returned the ladder to the storage room, they saw John Dean talking to a woman Davis recognized as Mary Jenkins. Davis and Bailey escorted her down the ramp to the sallyport area. She looked at the motor home from every angle, and finally said she couldn't be sure if it was the one she had seen because it was dark in the covered area. She also said the vehicle that had been on her road had a loud motor; she wanted to hear this one. Davis got the keys while Dean took down the crime-scene tape that surrounded the vehicle. He unlocked the vehicle and started the engine. After moving it to the middle of the parking lot, he got out and walked to where Jenkins and Dean were standing, about 75 feet away. This was about the same distance the witness had been from the vehicle when she saw it from her front porch. Jenkins confirmed that the sound of the motor was identical to the motor she'd heard on Saturday. She walked around the vehicle again and said the red birds on the sides were the same as she had remembered. She even remembered the flowered curtains in the windows.

The wind was blowing hard and it was threatening to rain. Dean escorted Jenkins inside the station to take her statement. Davis ran to the motor home, started the engine, and drove the vehicle into the sallyport. Moments later, the dark sky opened and poured but the motor home was safe and dry.

Later that morning, Tatum and Lamb drove the motor home to the Jefferson County Vehicle Maintenance Garage. They placed the vehicle on a hydraulic lift and raised it to the highest level. Davis and Lamb began to study the underside. Davis saw a black substance on the trailer hitch bolt that looked like asphalt. Was it asphalt from the north ramp of Cow Creek Bridge? Davis envisioned the vehicle descending the ramp. Because of the length of the vehicle from the rear tires to the bumper and trailer hitch, the lowest most extended part of the vehicle could have gouged the ramp, picking up the residue. He took a photo of the trailer hitch and the residue, and scraped it into a plastic bag.

The two identification experts found several interesting items in and around the undercarriage of Rex's motor home. Sand was wedged inside one of the braces on the back bumper, and on the fiberglass under the back end. The rest of the undercarriage was exceptionally clean. The three items of evidence had been found in uncommon areas that would not have been removed with just a general wash.

Rex Powell's motor home had now been examined for evidence inside and out. Tatum and Lamb left the county garage and drove the vehicle to the seizure lot behind the city fleet maintenance barn. The detectives parked and locked Rex Powell's motor home, but they had not seen the last of the large white vehicle with red stripes and flying birds.

The *Beaumont Enterprise* had publicized Lt. Coffin's request for witnesses who might have seen the motor home any time Saturday. The investigators could have imagined the response they would receive. As people read their Wednesday morning papers and saw the picture of Rex's motor home, police phones began to ring in Newton and Beaumont.

Nancy Bishop of Newton called and talked to Sheriff Powell. On Saturday, October 6, she, her daughter, and future son-in-law had gone to DeRidder, Louisiana about 10:00 a.m., to look at wedding gowns. As they approached the Sabine River Bridge, Bishop noticed a motor home stopped on the south side of Hwy. 190 at an old dirt logging road. The motor home accelerated and turned left onto the highway. Bishop recalled that the vehicle turned in front of her, forcing her to slow down to avoid hitting it. As the large vehicle turned left in front of her, Bishop was able to see red stripes and a red bird painted on it. After she crossed the bridge, Bishop passed the "slow poke" on its left side which also had red stripes and a red bird. Bishop did not see the driver, but her future son-in-law noticed that the driver was a white man who wore a mustache.

The second caller was Matilda Porterfield, a senior citizen who lived on Hwy. 1416. She had seen the strangely marked vehicle from her front porch as it headed south on her road.

Laurie Weathers had seen the motor home on that Saturday, too. Between 2:30 p.m. and 3:00 p.m. Saturday, she and her brother, David Jacks, had just passed the southernmost traffic light in Kirbyville, at the intersection of Hwy. 96 and Hwy. 1004, when David suddenly exclaimed, "There goes Rex!" Rex and Weathers' dad were friends, and David had seen Rex and his vehicle on several occasions when Rex would come by their house to visit. Weathers watched the motor home in her rear view mirror as it continued south-bound on Hwy. 96.

Davis called to talk to David Jacks and his dad. It just so happened that Saturday, October 6, was the first weekend of squirrel hunting season. Wayman Jacks and his son-in-law, Robert Weathers, decided to hunt after lunch. At the intersection of Hwy. 190 and Hwy. 1416, Jacks noticed a white motor home behind him turn left onto Hwy. 1416. He recognized the motor home as Rex Powell's. Jack noted the time: 1:30 p.m.

Yet another caller, Tammy Smith, was playing horse shoes at her friend Bill Aycock's house Saturday when they saw a motor home drive north past the house. Tammy saw the driver -- a white man with dark hair wearing glasses. As the vehicle went by, one of the friends commented, "If he keeps on going down *that* road, he's going to have a scratched up bird."

Tammy explained that Fox Hunters Club (known locally as Fox Hunter Road) becomes very narrow farther north and is heavily grown over with weeds and overhanging limbs. There were no through roads off Fox Hunter Road. The few dirt roads that intersected were dead-end trails that went to deer camps and hunting leases. A driver would have to continue north on Fox Hunter Road all the way to Hwy. 363, or turn around and go back to Hwy. 2460. The friends played horseshoes for most of the afternoon and never saw the motor home again. Tammy added that most people who drive on Fox Hunter Road are friendly, and will look over and wave. But the driver of the motor home was different. He did not even glance in their direction.

Deputy Whittaker had taken a short written statement from Judge Satterwhite on October 9 after Rex changed his story. The statement explained that Rex had come by Satterwhite's store between 3:45 p.m. and 4:30 p.m. that Saturday to see if any of his items had been sold at auction. Satterwhite remembered that Rex had been to see his in-laws in Merryville, and that they had not been home, so he had dropped by the store on his way back to Mauriceville. Satterwhite stated that Rex was driving the white motor home that day.

Davis decided to re-interview Judge Satterwhite. On October 23, Davis and Tatum went to Newton County and took sworn statements from Bishop, David and Wayman Jacks, and Judge Satterwhite. In his second statement, the judge narrowed the time of Rex's visit on October 6 to near 4:00 p.m. He had not seen which direction Rex had come from, but three people sitting in the store said Rex arrived eastbound on Hwy. 363 headed toward Louisiana. Rex had told the judge that he had just come *from* Louisiana.

Among the judge's other observations: he knew Rex had been injured and that he sometimes walked with a pronounced limp. But on this day, Satterwhite remembered Rex's limp was hardly noticeable. And, where Rex was usually jovial, joking, and cutting up with people, on October 6, he was not. He came in, asked his questions, and left.

The most significant sighting of the motor home that Saturday came from Roderick Lee Nelson, who had been squirrel hunting in a wooded area near his home. He came out of the woods between 12:30 and 1:30 p.m. As he walked along Hwy. 2460 toward his house he saw a white motor home with red stripes and a red bird on the side pass him going west. Roderick's sighting put Rex between Cow Creek Bridge and Mary Jenkins' road.

On October 11, Tatum, Davis, Bailey, and Coffin held a meeting in the police department's staff conference room. They decided that, beginning at Larry's Antique Mall, the motor home's route needed to be documented. Tatum suggested filming the route from the air with the assistance of the Texas Department of Public Safety's helicopter. The investigators also planned to take the motor home along the route to document driving time. The vehicle also needed to be driven back under the bridge to see if it would strike the support beams as measurements had indicated.

Friday morning, Tatum and Lamb boarded the D.P.S. helicopter at the Beaumont District Office. Lamb shot still photos of the areas where witnesses had seen the motor home, while Tatum filmed the areas with the video camera. The investigators also flew over the home of Rex's in-laws. From this perspective, it was surprising to see that there was not much distance between the old logging road where

Bishop had seen the motor home and the back of Rex's in-law's property. The helicopter headed back to Beaumont, flying over Rex's house in Mauriceville to take photos.

On October 15, Tatum and Bailey took the big white motor home on its presumed route. Tatum drove between fifty-five and sixty mph., changing speeds on the dirt roads. It took one hour and three minutes to drive from Larry's Antique Mall to the bridge over Hwy. 1416.

The officers took the motor home down the incline on the north side of Hwy. 1416, through the big mud hole, and to the spot under the bridge where Falyssa's body was found. Mud and sand fell off the back bumper. Following the tracks that were still evident in the sand, the investigators noted that the wheels of the motor home fit the tracks. Proceeding south, the air conditioner cowling struck the bridge, but in a difference place. The two officers attributed this discrepancy to speed and prior damage to the air conditioning unit. The officers timed the drive from Cow Creek Bridge to the dirt road on the Louisiana side of the Sabine River -- twenty-two minutes.

All in all, the trip with the motor home could not determine Rex's exact route on the afternoon of October 6, but it did confirm most of it, along with the times it took to go from place to place as the sightings had indicated.

Anticipating that Rex's motor home would be key evidence in court, the investigators also expected defense attorneys to insist that the motor home was not one-of-a-kind. Their goal: to create some element of doubt in just one juror's mind.

The vehicle registration showed that a man named David E. Prescott of DeRidder, Louisiana had owned the motor home before Rex. On Thursday October 25, Davis called Prescott, a self-employed sign painter and owner of Dave's Signs in DeRidder.

The drive to DeRidder was relaxing and pleasant. The sun was shining brightly, and the morning had been blessedly cool. Davis found Dave's Signs with no problem.

Prescott told Davis he bought the used motor home from a man in Leesville in the early 1970's. The vehicle was white, but had rust spots on it. Prescott painted and restored the vehicle to its original white color and, being a sign painter, he decided to decorate it. Using masking tape and red marine epoxy paint, he painted red stripes on both sides. Then with a sketch pad and a vivid imagination, Prescott sketched a design to fill the void past the side windows. He decided on a bird in flight.

Davis asked Prescott if he ever used that design on any other vehicle. "No," Prescott said. After he finished the bird design he threw his sketches away. Prescott was *positive* the design had not been used again. This information was almost too good to be true. Rex could have had an average nondescript motor home in brown, motor home beige or blue, with subtle markings. But he didn't. He had a one-of-a-kind, which meant that every sighting of the motor home was without a doubt Rex's vehicle, and his alone.

Before Davis left, Prescott added one last twist in his recollection of Rex and the motor home. When Rex and Corliss came to his house to look at the vehicle, it was filthy, and had not been driven in more than four years. But Rex wanted to buy it right away and asked Prescott if he could have the vehicle cleaned and running as soon as possible.

Prescott worked day and night to get the vehicle ready. Rex came back the next day to check on it. Prescott told Rex he was working as fast as he could and pointed out several things that were still not repaired. The problems didn't matter to Rex, and he wasn't interested in a test drive either. Prescott told the detectives he still wonders why Rex was so determined to possess the motor home in such short order. Davis's knowledge of sex crimes and growing evidence against Rex kicked his intuition into high gear. Were there other victims? If so, how many?

Powell's motor home in the police department's sallyport,
where investigators found damage to the top-mounted air
conditioner cowling consistent with scrapes found on the
underside of Cow Creek Bridge.

The rear of the motor home.

The plywood floor of Rex's motor home where
Falyssa's hair was found.

CHAPTER ELEVEN

FALYSSA'S FUNERAL

It was no small irony that on October 9, while Texas detectives were deeply involved in the busiest day of the investigation, Falyssa was quietly laid to rest in Louisiana. Beaumont and Newton County Investigators were working around the clock to nail down their case against Rex Powell, who had been arrested Sunday night. In Texas, more than a dozen officers answered telephones, interviewed witnesses, typed statements and drove back and forth between Beaumont and Cow Creek. At the same moment, a different mood engulfed Falyssa's family and friends just over the Sabine River in Lake Charles.

Elaine Langley never anticipated planning the funeral of one of her daughters, and certainly not under these circumstances. In little more than seventy-two hours, Falyssa had disappeared, her body had been found, her murderer arrested and her funeral held.

Thinking back, Elaine can remember some details of the funeral so vividly. Others fade into the fog that enveloped the family that hot October.

Sunday afternoon, Falyssa's body was released from the autopsy in Beaumont and transferred to Johnson Funeral Home in Lake Charles.

Next, the family had to face the gruesome physical aspects of Falyssa's death. As with most victims of strangulation, Falyssa's upper neck and face were swollen. Her face was hard to recognize because of the swelling. With so many children attending the funeral, an open casket was out of the question.

Elaine knew that Falyssa's beloved great-grandmother would not be able to accept the child's death without viewing the body. The family decided on a brief, private viewing by close family members.

On that damp Sunday afternoon, Elaine realized she needed a dress for Falyssa. A good friend who owns a local children's store opened it for the bereaved mother. Elaine selected a dress she thought Falyssa would have liked, an ivory Gunne Sax dress with lace and iridescent sequin trim. Elaine selected lacy socks and a purple headband, Falyssa's favorite color. Last but not least, Falyssa wore the beloved necklace and pewter pin which her first boyfriend, Chris, had given her a few days before her death.

With these difficult decisions made, the family had to focus on the stream of visitors who came to express their condolences and pay last respects to Falyssa. Among these were Falyssa's classmates. Some who attended and those who were not emotionally strong enough to attend had written letters to Falyssa. Elaine and Joe read each of them, then placed them in the casket, along with Falyssa's treasured pink "snow baby" doll.

The shocking nature of her murder had prompted administrators at F.K. White Elementary School to bring in a team of counselors to help the student body cope with the tragedy.

The weather on that day was foggy and overcast with an occasional light mist. Hundreds of people crowded into the funeral chapel for the 10:00 a.m. service. Flowers of every size and color imaginable provided the backdrop for Falyssa's golden casket emblazoned with pink carnations. On top Elaine had placed Falyssa's fifth-grade school picture.

Those who attended the funeral remember the outpouring of emotion not only because of the violent circumstances of Falyssa's death, but because of the presence in the chapel of so many children. The community had not had long to cope with this tragedy, and it all seemed to be happening so fast.

Falyssa was buried next to Elaine's mother who died when Falyssa was eight months old. The graveside service was for immediate family and a few close friends only. Elaine and Joe said their final goodbyes.

Even today, visitors to Falyssa's grave site are struck by the uniqueness of her headstone. Falyssa's portrait, hand-painted on porcelain, is set in a locket style frame next to a bronze unicorn. On the right of the marker is a symbol some people might not recognize.

The "Infant of Prague" depiction of Jesus had special significance to Falyssa. She had always been enthralled by the religious image on a night light at her great-grandmother's house. Some months before Falyssa died, her great-grandmother had given her the light. Falyssa never went to sleep without it, and called it her "Little King" because of the figure's regal robes.

Next to Falyssa's name on the headstone, her mother chose to place the image of the "Infant of Prague." Under the child's name was the inscription, "With Her Little King Forever."

(Later, Elaine would remember that from the time Falyssa had received the night light, she never turned it off, even in the daytime. After the funeral, almost without thinking, Elaine entered her daughter's room and turned off the light forever.)

People visit Falyssa's grave regularly, leaving behind fresh flowers or personal mementos for the child. In the weeks that followed Falyssa's death, Elaine and Joe received many messages of sympathy. One tribute was especially poignant. Falyssa's friend, Cecily Morgan, wrote a poem that captured Falyssa's energetic personality and sweet spirit in the way only another innocent child could express it.

FALYSSA

Flowers, sunshine and
  the stars above.
These are the things
  Falyssa loved.

A field of flowers,
  that I see.
Always remind me
  of her sweet and cheerful
Personality.

Her smile was like
  the sun.
That shone brightly
  when she was having fun.

The stars at night winking,
  those are her eyes twinkling.
Looking down at all the people
  that she loves.
She is OUR angel from above.

Someday, forever and ever,
  We will be in a big family
All together.

Until that time,
  the memory of her
Lingers on my mind.

By
CECILY MORGAN
Age 11
1991

Still today, visitors to Falyssa's gravesite leave behind
flowers and personal mementoes..

In memory

FALYSSA ANN VAN WINKLE

Funeral services for Falyssa Ann Van Winkle, 10, daughter of Joe and Elaine Langley and Michael and Julie Van Winkle, all of Lake Charles, will be at 10 a.m. Tuesday, Oct. 9, in Johnson Funeral Home.

Burial will be in Consolata Cemetery.

Miss Van Winkle died Saturday, Oct. 6, 1990, in Texas.

A lifelong resident of Lake Charles, she was a sixth-grade student at F.K. White Elementary.

Survivors are her parents; one sister, Shonna Van Winkle; two stepsisters, Helen and Connie Cody; two stepbrothers, Jason and Tim Cody; maternal grandfather, Martin LeVergne; paternal grandmother, Carol Ann Van Winkle; paternal stepgrandparents, Jim and Nancy Madison and Mr. and Mrs. Carl Steen Coco, all of Lake Charles; maternal great-grandmother, Erzil Sonnier of Rayne, and paternal great-grandparents, Mr. and Mrs. Stanley Ward of Sanford, Fla.

CHAPTER TWELVE

MORE VICTIMS

People like Rex Powell don't commit one crime and then get caught. Usually they have committed a number of crimes over a period of time. They "get away with it" over time by some combination of cunning, deceit, or terrorism. They get caught when they get too sure of themselves. They get lax in the planning or act too instinctively when a victim or opportunity presents itself, and when something goes wrong -- they get caught.

Rex Powell's arrest record showed multiple charges from one incident with no conviction. Davis's instincts told him there had to be more incidents in which formal charges were not filed. He thought of the countless cases he'd worked where a specific man had raped a woman or molested a child but was never brought to justice because of lack of evidence or probable cause. In the case of Falyssa Van Winkle, the evidence and the background were there for a conviction. Davis might never know how many crimes Rex had committed, but he did know one thing -- he was going to make sure that little Falyssa was his last.

Leads in a case can come from anywhere, and often out of nowhere. Most usually come from the general direction an investigator is headed, then unfold, with one lead revealing another until a case is solved. This was an exception. As Davis pondered this, Officer Jerry LaChance knocked on the investigators open door. LaChance had relatives in the Merryville, Louisiana area who had knowledge of Rex's past. Davis listened intently as the patrolman shed light on another chapter of Rex's past.

LaChance's relatives had disclosed that Rex's wife, Corliss had a sister, Lucy* with a fourteen-year-old daughter, Cindy.* At age twelve, Cindy had been sexually assaulted in her home by a masked man she thought was Rex. Deputy Robert McCullough of the Beauregard Parish Sheriff's Department investigated the case but it was never solved. As a routine part of her investigation, the girl had been given a sexual assault examination at a hospital. Davis noted that the kit might be available for analysis. Rex had been listed as a possible suspect but no arrest had ever been made, in part, because Corliss' family had kept the child from investigating officers.

In another startling revelation, LaChance told Davis that the victim of Rex's 1984 burglary, attempted rape, and attempted murder was an elderly lady named Lucille Jackson, who still lived in the Merryville area and would love to be interviewed.

LaChance continued: Rex and Corliss had one child, a daughter named Nancy*, who had married a few months earlier. Jerry said she had told people that Rex had molested her since she was ten-years old, with the last incident occurring just two months before she was married. LaChance had it on good authority that, one night, when Corliss was at work, Rex had tried to molest Nancy. She fought off his attack and managed to call her fiancé. He came to her rescue and she lived with his parents until they were married.

LaChance was a literal encyclopedia of information about James Rexford Powell. Rex's dad was Marvin Powell, who lived near Fort Polk Army Base in Louisiana. His mother was Germaine Powell who supposedly lived near Pickering, Louisiana. Rex had three brothers: Frances, Jerry, and Ben, and two sisters: Roxanne and Bridgette.

Before he left, Jerry LaChance volunteered one last piece of information: three or four girls had been reported missing from the Merryville-DeRidder-Fort Polk area in recent years. Two of them had been found dead, and no one has been arrested.

Joe Langley called Davis on October 10 to say he had heard from a woman, Kay Williams, who offered to help investigators locate Rex and Corliss' daughter, Nancy*. Williams went on to say that Rex and Corliss had only lived in Mauriceville for about eight or nine months.

Before that they had lived in the Merryville area close to Corliss' parents, Dexter* and Virginia* Jones.

This lead continued to produce information against Rex. Kay said that since Nancy was a little girl, she had told Virginia and Corliss that her Daddy had been touching and "messing" with her. But Virginia had told the child she'd just had a bad dream.

Davis thought of the many times children had told him how they've cried out for help to someone they trusted only to be brushed off as a bad dream or malicious lie. Some children had even been punished for telling of their victimization. He thought of the times he's had to reassure the innocent creatures that someone believed them. These thoughts simply fueled Davis' fire as he reached for the phone to call Nancy.

Davis told Nancy's husband that the police knew about his wife's molestation. But Nancy was not home; she was at her grandmother's house. Davis asked if Nancy would talk to him if he called her at Virginia's. Jim, who probably knew as many of Rex's secrets as Rex's own daughter, haltingly explained that his wife's grandmother was a very headstrong woman who tightly ruled her roost, and that Nancy would not talk, nor would anyone talk, about Rex or anything else around Virginia. Davis arranged to call Nancy the next day.

When Davis said hello to Rex's daughter, she remained silent. He told her he would like to talk to her about the things her dad had done to her. Nancy asked the detective what was he talking about, hoping he would accept her ignorance and drop the subject. He told her he knew about her being molested by her father. "How did you know about that?" she asked. Davis told her he knew she'd tried to tell her grandmother but had been ignored. Davis assured her that even though Virginia had refused to believe her or listen to her, he did believe her and wanted to talk to her in person. She agreed to come to his office in about an hour and a half. It was 9:00 a.m.

More than three hours later, the young couple walked through the door to the Special Crimes Bureau lobby. The detectives immediately sensed that Jim was uncomfortable. Nancy was downright scared. The officers tried to calm Nancy but she could not regain her composure and the interview ended about 1:30 p.m. with Nancy having said little. She would neither confirm nor deny her father's molestation. Who had instilled such fear in Nancy? The answer walked out of the Beaumont Police Station and headed back to Merryville, locked deeply inside a tormented young woman.

Davis knew Nancy was not the only alleged victim of Rex Powell. He remembered the 1989 sexual assault of Rex's twelve-year-old niece, Cindy, and the fire in Cindy's parents' home in 1986, and the fire at Rex's own home in 1985. Both fires were of suspicious origin. Then there was Lucille Jackson.

One investigator had seen Rex Powell slip away from justice more times than most criminals deal with the justice system -- Beauregard Parish Sheriff's Deputy Robert McCullough. Davis called the Louisiana lawman as soon as he arrived for work Friday, October 12.

"Do you have enough to convict him this time?" McCullough asked. Davis assured him Rex had committed his last crime. Davis said that he'd like to talk to Cindy to see if she would come forward and testify that Rex had been the one who raped her (if this allegation was true). McCullough said he'd call her mother, Lucy, and ask to talk to the girl. Davis and Don Bailey left for Louisiana.

Arriving at the rendezvous point -- a funeral home parking lot in Merryville -- Davis and Bailey met McCullough, who did not have good news. Lucy had not been happy about her daughter's case being brought up again, and had refused permission for the men to talk to Cindy. Lucy said Cindy had "forgotten" all about the incidents and she wanted it to stay that way.

In Cindy's case, McCullough had immediately suspected

Rex. The physical description of the suspect was about the same as Rex, and the voice was similar to the voice of her uncle even though the suspect had tried to disguise his voice. Cindy initially thought it was Rex but was not able to make a firm identification prior to her mother and grandmother quashing the investigation.

McCullough still had Cindy's sexual assault evidence samples, preserved for over a year in his department's evidence refrigerator. Davis now had Rex's blood. On an upcoming trip to Washington D.C., to deliver evidence on Falyssa's case for DNA analysis, Davis agreed also to take Cindy's rape kit.[2]

As for the suspicious fires, McCollough recalled that Rex was again the top suspect. Rex was reportedly seen around his house May 25, 1985 even though he was supposedly at the family's camp at the lake. Arson was highly suspected, but the insurance company paid anyway under threat of litigation. McCullough said rumor had it that Rex used the money to pay his lawyer to defend him in the attempted rape and attempted capital murder trial of Lucille Jackson in 1985.

Lucy's house fire was equally suspicious. It had occurred on July 19, 1986, and Rex Powell was the person who called the fire deparment. A rumor again circulated that Rex had been in the area of the house just before the fire. Both fires had begun from elecrical problems, and in both cases, insurance paid the damage in full, even though the fires were suspicious.

McCullough wrapped up his rundown of Rex Powell cases. He and Davis left to pay a visit to Dexter and Virginia Jones.

---

[2]   Unfortunately, authorities later learned that the biological evidence had deteriorated and could not be DNA tested for comparison purposes.

Clad in overalls and a long-sleeved plaid cotton shirt, a man stepped off the porch of the old frame house. Dexter Jones told the detectives that Virginia and Corliss had gone into town. The detectives expected Virginia to thwart any interview, so they thought they might have gotten lucky with Virginia away from the house.

"Mr. Jones," Davis began, "What do you think about the case against Rex?" The elderly man shrugged his shoulders and said he didn't know, then added, "Rex is a peculiar person. One day he would talk your ears off, and the next day he wouldn't say two words to you." Davis asked Jones if he would describe Rex as moody and the old man replied, "Yeah."

Davis asked him where he had been on Saturday, October 6. Jones said he and Virginia and a couple of their grandchildren had gone to the hunting camp on Friday and that he had hunted on Saturday morning. After the Joneses got home around 1:30 p.m., Rex never came by. In fact, his father-in-law had not seen Rex in about a month.

Falyssa in kindergarten.

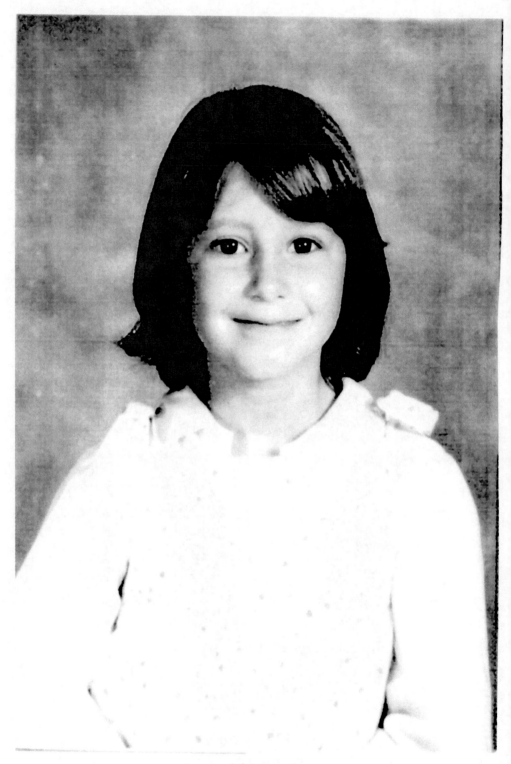

A proud first-grader.

CHAPTER THIRTEEN

MRS. LUCILLE JACKSON

Lucille Jackson lived in a remote area outside Merryville, Louisiana, but it was not difficult to find her immaculate, white, wood-framed house. After listing the highways and roads, she told guests to "look for the cleanest pasture, and turn just past the only fence on the highway without trash and litter." It was a description that led directly to her home.

Mrs. Jackson carried herself well. After all, she was only "sixty-six-years young" in August 1984, at the time of her fateful encounter with Rex Powell. Her snow-white hair glistened, framing a constant smile. She was somewhat thin, her hands and face worn from years of hard work, yet gentle to the touch. Her attire was always simple: cotton gingham dress, head scarf, and black knee-high rubber boots.

She arose at 4:30 a.m., as usual, on what was to become an unforgettable August morning in 1984. Knowing she would be hungry when she finished her morning chores, Mrs. Jackson started fixing her lunch as soon as she finished milking Blue Bell, her faithful cow. Suddenly she heard a vehicle coming up her driveway. She looked up to see her only grandchild, twelve-year-old Cary, driving his dad's truck the short distance to her house. Cary walked over and gave his grandmother a big hug and kiss, which thrilled her, because this young man was her pride and joy. He gathered the gardening tools he had come to borrow, kissed his grandmother again, and drove away.

The "old homestead" was a couple of hundred yards south of her place. The house was solidly built and still standing though it had been vacant since the death of Mrs. Jackson's parents many years earlier. The open dog-trot wood frame house reflected the simple country architecture of the turn of the century. A tin roof, front porch swing, and picket fence enclosing the front yard rounded out the classic country setting.

Mrs. Jackson completed her household chores that August

morning and decided to go to the old place and do some work. Everything needed repair. Lucille had replaced decayed fence posts and rusty barbed wire for days on end. Poverty weeds had taken over, and she had begun digging up the huge roots with a hoe. August 2, 1984, was no different. She had to get a few more dug.

Mrs. Jackson got into her 1964 Chevrolet pickup truck and drove to the property of her daughter and son-in-law, Myrna and Junior Cooley, who were building a house. Mrs. Jackson visited with the two for a few minutes before returning to her labor of love at the old place. Cars were constantly passing on the highway, but she paid no attention to them as she worked at the task at hand. Occasionally a vehicle would pass and honk, the occupants recognizing the sweet lady as she toiled in the yard. She'd always look up, smile, and wave, recognizing most of the people greeting her.

About 10:00 a.m. a vehicle approached with a louder than usual sound that caught her attention. As it came into sight she saw that it was a yellow Jeep-type vehicle with no top driven by a white man with a brown beard who was wearing a blue shirt and cap. The vehicle passed but returned shortly.

She finished her work and a few minutes later, winning the battle of the weeds for the moment. She returned home and served lunch to Cary before turning her attention to the daily chores around her place. She walked to the back porch, slipped off her canvas shoes and stepped back into her rubber boots. She walked to the barn, filled a bucket with range meal and headed to the pasture to feed her cows. As she walked the fence row toward the highway, she heard the same strange-sounding vehicle she'd heard earlier, this time headed toward her on the highway. As it approached, she saw that it was the same man and vehicle that she'd seen earlier in the day. As he passed, the driver waved.

A short time later when Lucille was in the house preparing to wash her hair, she thought she heard the same vehicle drive around to the back of her house. She walked onto her back porch and saw the open-top yellow sport utility vehicle parked by her backyard gate. The white man with the beard had already come through the gate, and was walking toward her house. She stepped outside the screen door. She walked out into her backyard, meeting the man at the tree near her back door.

Mrs. Jackson immediately had an odd feeling that all was not right. The man said he had been looking at the timber on her property and asked if she'd be interesting in selling it. She told the man she wasn't interested. He started walking back to his vehicle and she turned to go back in the house.

As she reached the bottom of her back door steps, the stranger grabbed her by the neck and shoulders and pushed her into the house. He dragged her across the screened-in back porch and through the kitchen. When he showed her a small black pistol that fit easily inside the palm of his hand, she said, "What are you doing to me?" With terror in his eyes and voice he said, "Lady, this is it. I am going to rape you. If you do what I want you to, I won't kill you." Mrs. Jackson knew better. She'd seen his face. She knew what he looked like and could identify him. Mrs. Jackson was not one to give up without a struggle. She was fighting, kicking, and screaming in the hope that someone might hear her desperate call.

After the attacker dragged her into her bedroom, he tried to pull her from the floor onto the bed. Pure, blind, bonafide fear took hold of Lucille Jackson. The adrenaline pumping through her body increased her strength more than any man could have imagined. Her attacker couldn't maintain control over her and hold onto his gun, too. He laid the gun on the bed and gave up the idea of getting her on the bed to rape her -- he would rape her on the floor beside the bed. She was still fighting so hard he could not remove her clothes. He ripped open the front of her dress, but could not undo his clothes to carry out the sexual assault because she was fighting so hard.

He grabbed a dress that Mrs. Jackson had laid on the bed,

wrapped it around her neck, and began to pull hard. Her fingers grabbed at the material. She pushed with her feet and managed to get her head under the bed, lessening the man's leverage on the noose. She quickly rolled into a fetal position, praying for a miracle, when a shot rang out. A piercing pain shot through the left side of her head as blood began to pour from her eye and nose. She tried to push herself under the bed even more. Pain ripped through her again as her attacker struck her on the back of the head. Unconsciousness was suddenly a bittersweet peace.

Mrs. Jackson awoke to hear the man's vehicle starting. Her body was wracked with pain but her head felt as if it had exploded. She could not see out of her left eye. She couldn't hear out of her left ear. But she was alive. He had left her for dead but she was alive. Slowly raising her head from a pool of blood, Mrs. Jackson managed to get to her knees. She steadied herself on the bed and pulled herself to her feet. As she staggered to the door she heard the Jeep take off toward the highway.

With blood covering her face, she stumbled over her .12 gauge shotgun lying on the floor. She realized this must have been what he'd used to hit her in the back of the head. Staggering to her living room, she grabbed for the phone, but saw that it had been ripped from the wall.

Weak and disorientated, she was determined to survive, and headed for her truck. She drove to the old place, only to find Junior and Cary gone. With failing strength, Mrs. Jackson turned her truck around and headed across the highway. She was blowing the truck horn with all her might as she approached Margaret Thomas's house. Margaret ran out to greet her, but instead of seeing the warm face of her friend that was always aglow and full of life, Margaret saw blood pouring from the left side of Mrs. Jackson's face. Her friend could not imagine what had happened.

Margaret Thomas summoned an ambulance and the police. Mrs. Jackson's prayers had been answered. She was rushed to the hospital with the police chief at her side. No one could hurt her now. She had not been raped and she was alive.

The Merryville emergency room physician determined that she was shot point-blank in the left ear and the bullet had traveled just inside the skull, then exited through the left eye socket. Amazingly, this was done without damage to her brain. She had been lucky, extremely lucky. Or, maybe luck had nothing to do with it at all. Maybe God still had plans for Lucille Jackson.

After Mrs. Jackson was stabilized and transferred to a larger hospital in Lake Charles, Merryville Police Chief Louis Cooper summoned help from the Beauregard Parish Sheriff's Department. Deputies first inspected Mrs. Jackson's home, finding the tell-tale trail of blood that would lead them from the driveway to Mrs. Jackson's bedroom. They found four-wheel-drive mud-grip tire tracks in the dirt driveway, of which they made imprints for later investigation.

Inside they found the disconnected phone; a .12 gauge shotgun with blood stains on it and several pieces of broken glass mingled with a large pool of blood on the bedroom floor. Deputy McCullough would later have the fragments of glass analyzed, but he knew they were from the left corrective lens of Mrs. Jackson's eyeglasses. The lens had been shattered as the bullet exited her eye socket. Mixed in with the broken glass, Robert found another piece of evidence -- the bullet. It was small, obviously from a small-caliber gun. But it had almost been big enough, he thought, to take the life of Mrs. Jackson.

As the lawmen were leaving Mrs. Jackson's house, the dispatcher told them a Mr. Cornwell had called the Sheriff's Department. He had heard about Mrs. Jackson's attack, and had some information about the suspect. The investigators traveled immediately to the Cornwell residence. They learned that the Sunday before Mrs. Jackson's attack, a man matching the description of her assailant had come to the Cornwell house. The man told Cornwell that he was looking for a fifth-wheel to put on his truck to haul a load of logs. Mr. Cornwell described the man as being about five feet seven inches tall and weighing about 160-170 pounds, with a sandy colored full beard. The man had been driving a muddy yellow open-top Jeep-type vehicle. The detective thanked

Cornwell for such a thorough description, but the witness had a startling finale. He and his son *knew* the man. His name was Rex Powell. Elated, but cautious, the two deputies now had a lead with a name.

It was a busy afternoon for the detectives. They immediately had another call placing a man matching Rex Powell's description in the vicinity of Mrs. Jackson's residence within minutes of her assault. Measurements showed that it was only 1.8 miles from Mrs. Jackson's house to Rex's house. Even on winding country roads that short distance could be driven in less than two minutes. The lawmen agreed it was time to visit Rex Powell.

No one was at home when the detectives arrived, but a 1977 Toyota four-wheel drive Land Cruiser was parked in the front yard. The vehicle was yellow and had no doors or top. It clearly resembled a Jeep-type vehicle.

While the deputies were looking over the Land Cruiser a vehicle turned into the driveway. A man, woman and young girl exited the vehicle and approached the four lawmen. Deputy Ace Schiro had been the prinicipal of Merryville High School when Rex Powell graduated in 1964, and he immediately recognized Rex.

After introductions to the other officers, Rex was asked what happened to his beard. He explained, in a natural manner (according to the lawmen, "so natural it was scary") that he had been at his mother-in-law's house when he'd heard about Mrs. Jackson's incident, including the description of the suspect and his vehicle. Rex said he immediately shaved his beard because the description sounded so much like him that people might mistake him for the suspect. He told the detectives that he wasn't going to drive the Land Cruiser anymore, either. Rex then volunteered a rough itinerary of his day's activities and ended it by saying that Mrs. Jackson knew him and should be able to tell the detectives that he was not the person who had attacked her.

With that in mind, the detectives had Mrs. Jackson contacted at the hospital. Stabilized but still in great pain, Mrs. Jackson identified Rex Powell as the attacker. She specifically recalled the distinctive eyes of the Powell family -- a trait shared by Rex and his father, a former Merryville school custodian. She had gotten a very good look at her attacker's eyes as he tried to choke the life out of her, and she assured everyone that she would never forget "those eyes."

The detectives returned to Rex Powell's home less than two hours after their first visit. Rex was read his rights and signed a form permitting officers to search his property and seize evidence. Authorities seized the clothes Rex had worn that day and two small pistols. They also examined and photographed the vehicle tires and tread design, noting the wear patterns were similar to the tracks in Mrs. Jackson's yard. (This was confirmed by a local tire expert's comparison of the plaster casts with Rex Powell's tires.) The request by the investigators for Rex to come to the station and give a written statement was declined when Rex consulted a local attorney.

Meanwhile, a number of other local residents identified the yellow Jeep-type vehicle in the vicinity at the time and Rex Powell as its driver. Several citizens also gave information about a .25 caliber semi-automatic pistol Rex had shown them several times in recent months.

Based on this evidence, a local district court issued an evidentiary search warrant against Rex Powell's person. Among the items taken were hair and blood samples. As soon as she was able, Mrs. Jackson participated in both a photo and live lineup, that latter with voice identification as well.

In each lineup, Mrs. Jackson singled out Rex Powell.

On August 9, exactly one week after Lucille Jackson's attack, three warrants were issued for the arrest of James Rexford Powell. He was charged with aggravated burglary, attempted aggravated rape, and attempted first degree murder.

The trial against Rex Powell began seven months later, on

March 18, 1985, in the District Court of Beauregard Parish, Louisiana. Several corroborative witnesses testified for the state before Lucille Jackson took the stand. She recounted the attack and positively identified Rex Powell as the perpetrator. The defense attorney was not able to shake her identification of Rex Powell in the least.

The defense called Rex Powell as its first witness. It was not a surprise that he admitted he had known Mrs. Jackson all his life, but he denied that he attacked her. What was a surprise was the limited and subdued cross-examination by the state.

Most prosecutors relish any opportunity to vigorously cross-examine a criminal defendant, particularly one with Rex Powell's baggage. The onlookers who thought the prosecutor missed irreplaceable opportunities to question Powell's "alibi" were even more dismayed at the state's cross-examination of Justice Neely. Powell's uncle by marriage, he was the bondsman on the case for a total bond of $135,000.

On direct examination for the defense, Neely told of sitting on his screened-in porch on the south side of his house at the approximate time of Mrs. Jackson's assault. Neely said he had a completely unobstructed view of the highway leading to Mrs. Jackson's house, and saw a yellow Jeep with a cloth top headed toward Mrs. Jackson's house. Neely said the vehicle was driven by a white, dirty-looking, long haired male with a beard who was *not* Rex Powell. He said he would have recognized Rex Powell because they had known each other for a long time.

Despite numerous witnesses placing Rex Powell near the scene, the prosecutor never asked Neely if he had seen Rex Powell that day, which turned out to be a fatal error.

Neely's questions and answers gave the impression that only one yellow Jeep driven by an unknown white male was seen traveling near Mrs. Jackson's house that afternoon by Justice Neely or anyone else -- the creation of reasonable doubt. This infuriated some onlookers, who knew better. Also, the family could not believe that the prosecutor had not questioned Neely's ability to see the driver. A lot of people in the community had visited Justice Neely's house and knew that his view was severely obstructed by shrubbery on that side of the house.

Mrs. Jackson had been present for the entire trial, but was too exhausted to stay for the deliberations which began at 5:30 p.m. Friday. Her daughter, Myrna, stayed for the verdict, and was devastated by "Not Guilty" findings on all counts.

Many other Merryville residents were shocked by Rex Powell's acquittal in a case where the victim and so many eye witnesses identified the defendant. Several possible answers emerged over time, most of them political. For example, between Rex Powell's arrest and trial, the prosecuting attorney ran for re-election. One of his most ardent supporters was the same Justice Neely who had testified at trial on behalf of Rex Powell. After Powell was arrested but before the election, Neely hosted a fund raiser for the district attorney and many who attended were related to Rex Powell or shared his last name. Was this why Justice Neely was not challenged on the stand by the prosecutor?

Mrs. Jackson and her family had been somewhat concerned during the trial at what they considered to be a lackluster prosecution -- particularly the cross-examination of Rex Powell and Justice Neely. When the family learned that Rex Powell had displayed campaign signs in his yard for the man who would prosecute him only a few months later, they were aghast at the political overtones. Mrs. Jackson and her family considered Rex Powell a violent man who would commit other, similar crimes -- especially after he got away with attempted murder.

Sadly, at least one of the jurors had the same fear even as the jury acquitted Rex Powell in Mrs. Jackson's case. Jill Kelly* was in the minority of jurors who believed Rex Powell was guilty, and she and others wept as they were persuaded to vote not guilty so they would not have a hung jury. Kelly recalled that the majority of jurors felt that the prosecutor had not tried a very good case. He was seriously "out-lawyered" by Powell's defense attorney, and his case was irreparably damaged by Justice Neely's unchallenged testimony. Kelly had lingering regrets about the verdict, and her worst night-mare came true five years later on October 8, 1990, when, in her car, she heard the news that Rex Powell had been arrested in Texas in connection with the kidnapping, rape, and murder of a ten-year-old girl. Kelley later told Davis that she had trouble staying on the road as she was overcome by sadness and guilt. She couldn't help but feeling some responsibility for the girl's death. If Rex had been convicted and given even a moderate sentence, he would have not been free to kill Falyssa.

There were changes for other participants in Rex Powell's 1984 trial. The prosecutor, who had narrowly defeated his opponent in November 1984 (with the assistance of Justice Neely and the Powell family), declined to run for re-election in 1990. The prosecutor's political strength had apparently waned, as the candidate he supported as his successor was handily defeated.

As for Justice Neely, just before the start of the Texas trial for Falyssa's death in 1991, he gave a sworn statement about the 1984 incident involving Mrs. Jackson. (Texas investigators had already learned that Justice Neely had lost his bonding company, in part, because he never received all of his fee from Rex Powell.)

Neely swore that he told the truth to the question he had been asked on the witness stand in 1985. But after Falyssa's gruesome death, Neely said that he had *seen* Rex drive by his house headed away from the direction of Mrs. Jackson's house on the afternoon of August 2, 1984.

Perplexed investigators asked Neely why he had not mentioned this critical fact in the 1985 trial. Justice Neely simply said that no one had asked him that question. Neely insisted that he had seen two yellow Jeeps go past his house that August afternoon, and he had only been asked about one of them.

When faced with the implication that his own testimony had set Rex free to murder Falyssa, Neely responded that it was up to the prosecutor to ask him the right questions and the prosecutor did not do so. This was little consolation for Lucille Jackson and her family, and even less for Falyssa's family. They thought it abhorrent that this man's first name was "Justice," because in their minds he had perpetuated a mockery of justice that cost Falyssa her life.

In time, Mrs. Jackson learned to cope with the permanent injuries from the gun shot. Surgeons repaired what they could, but she lost all hearing in her left ear and had to endure a glass eye on the left side. Through it all, however, she didn't lose her spirit or love of life. Although she had lost *her* day in court, she would have an opportunity very few victims ever see -- a second day in court. Rex Powell had not seen the last of Lucille Jackson.

Lucille Jackson with grandson, Cary, and the 1964-model truck she drove for help after her attack in 1984.

Mrs. Jackson, age 76, hoeing weeds in her pasture, 1993.

Her friends, Sport the cat and Coo-Coo the guinea hen,
accompany Lucille Jackson on her daily chores.

Lucille Jackson on the front porch of her
Merryville, Louisiana, home.

CHAPTER FOURTEEN

GETTING READY

The Texas Code of Criminal Procedure states that a person charged with the crime of murder or capital murder must be tried in the county where the crime was committed. The Code further states that if the exact location of death cannot be determined, venue for the trial becomes the county where the body was found. This put the trial squarely in the prosecuting jurisdiction of Charles Ramsey Mitchell, District Attorney of Sabine, Newton, and San Augustine Counties. A lifelong resident of San Augustine, Mitchell had deep and respected roots in the East Texas community.

Capital murder requires specific elements. In this case, no one had seen Rex kidnap Falyssa. No one had seen her in his motor home. No one had seen him rape or kill the little girl. But, hopefully, Rex had left a part of himself behind at the crime scene; the crime scene inside Falyssa's body.

This made the autopsy rape kit evidence crucial to the prosecution. In the Jefferson County Regional Crime Lab, Technician Phyllis Marshall greeted McWilliams, Hobbs, and identification expert Sue Kelly. McWilliams asked Marshall to analyze the vaginal swab slides for the presence of semen.

Later that afternoon, Phyllis called McWilliams with the results. Rex Powell had tried to cover all of his tracks, but he had not been able to destroy everything. He had left his DNA fingerprints behind. There was more than enough semen present on the slides to conduct DNA testing.

Now that it was decided *where* to try Rex Powell, thoughts turned to issues of *how* to try the "Mayor of Mauriceville." Mitchell felt this could be a strong DNA case. Although he had successfully prosecuted several murder cases, he had never prosecuted one where the use of DNA evidence was a focal point. The prosecutors agreed that McWilliams would lead in presenting the laboratory evidence because of his experience in this area.

But what type of jurors might they encounter in Newton County? Some communities as a whole do not believe in the death penalty, while others believed "an eye for an eye." Mitchell had a good feel for his constituents in deep East Texas. "It's a good place for a prosecution jury," he promised.

This trial was going to be a positive challenge for the collective intelligence, experience, and determination of the aggressive prosecutors. In short, Rex Powell didn't stand a chance.

That afternoon, the "Mayor of Mauriceville's" address changed. He was transferred from the Jefferson County Jail, eighty miles north, to the Newton County Jail.

On Thursday morning, November 8, a caravan traveled from Jefferson County to give testimony before the Newton County Grand Jury hearing evidence against Rex Powell.

After testimony from the numerous investigators from Newton County, Beaumont Police Department, and the Jefferson County District Attorney's Office, there was no doubt about the grand jury's decision. The indictment was handed down and the *State of Texas vs. James Rexford Powell* was assigned to the district court of Judge Bob Golden. Rex Powell would have his day in court, again.

Fun-loving Falyssa enjoys a summer swimming party, 1984

CHAPTER FIFTEEN

A TRIP TO D.C.

Things finally began to settle down the second week after Rex's arrest. All of the evidence that could be seized had been seized. Most of the detectives who worked on the investigation during its critical first few days had turned in their final supplementary reports and were now working on other cases. Frank Coffin assigned to Bill Davis the task of completing the investigation.

On October 16, in a large conference room at the station, detectives spread the evidence on top of an oversized table. The majority of it would be analyzed by the experts at the F.B.I Laboratory in Washington, D.C. The rest would go to Cellmar Diagnostics Lab in nearby Germantown, Maryland, for DNA analysis. One trip would take care of it all.

The F.B.I mandates that a specific list of evidence and requested tests accompany items of evidence. Tatum and McWilliams prepared the background then categorized known and unknown samples into three groups -- hair samples, soil and material samples, and fiber samples.

Hair Samples
1. Pulled and cut head hair from victim
2. Combed pubic hair from victim
3. Pulled pubic hair from victim
4. Combed pubic hair from James Rexford Powell
5. Pulled pubic hair from James Rexford Powell
6. Combed head hair from James Rexford Powell
7. Pulled head hair from James Rexford Powell
8. Hair from T-shirt of victim
9. Hair from left cheek of victim
10. Hair from left shoulder of victim
11. Hair from back of victim
12. Hair near rear exit of motor home
13. Hair from passenger side of motor home

14. Hair found in center of motor home
15. Hair found on right cushion of motor home
16. Hair found on driver's side window of motor home
17. Hair and soil sample from driver's side door
18. Hair from driver's side

Soiled Material
1.   Soil sample from crime scene
2.   Soil sample from crime scene
3.   Sand sample from crime scene
4.   Sand sample from crime scene
5.   Sand sample from crime scene
6.   Sand sample from crime scene
7.   Asphalt sample from crime scene
8.   Asphalt sample from crime scene
9.   Soil from passenger side of motor home
10. Soil from front bumper of motor home
11. Soil from rear bumper brace of motor home
12. Soil from under motor home
13. Soil from rear bumper of motor home
14. License plate from motor home
15. Asphalt from trailer hitch of motor home

Fiber Samples
1.   Two ropes from body of victim
2.   Three pieces of rope found at crime scene
3.   Knife taken from James Rexford Powell
4.   Portable vacuum cleaner and contents from residence of James Rexford Powell

That afternoon Tatum placed the envelopes and plastic bags into a brown accordion folder. All was in order for the trip to D.C.

Thanks to the efforts of Bob Wortham, the United States Attorney for the Eastern District of Texas at the time, the Beaumont Police

Department had a 1979 Cessna Turbo 210 Centurion. This was a Cadillac single-engine airplane that had been confiscated from drug smugglers.

Wednesday morning October 17 was a delightful morning for flying. Department Pilots Lt. Bill Conley and Sgt. Mike Lane received an all-clear weather bulletin all the way to the East Coast. With their passengers, Frank Coffin and Bill Tatum, they climbed to an elevation of 10,000 feet. Conley adjusted the instruments for a cruising speed of 175 knots or 190 m.p.h. They were on their way.

Three hours later Beaumont Police Department's *Air One* landed at Maness, Maryland located between D.C. and Germantown.

Following a delicious supper and a good night's rest the four officers traveled to the Cellmark Diagnostic Laboratory in Germantown. Coffin turned over the two rape kits and the vials of blood to the technician, and exchanged the required information for the tests to be conducted.

Tatum had been to FBI Headquarters in the J. Edgar Hoover Building before, but was still impressed by the sheer size of the building. The officers asked for Agent Doug Deedrick, a hair and fiber expert. After a brief tour, Tatum handed over to Deedrick the brown accordion folder.

Deedrick removed one of the hairs from the envelope that was marked "Falyssa Van Winkle." He then removed an unknown sample -- one found on Rex's plywood floor. He put both hairs on clear glass slides and placed them under a powerful microscope. Deedrick raised his eyes from the lens and smiled. The hairs were a match. This one piece of microscopic evidence put Falyssa inside Rex's motor home. But Deedrick had even more to tell. He told them that the hair had been forcibly removed from her scalp.

Notified in Beaumont, Davis couldn't keep this explosive news to himself. Now everyone *knew* that the right man had been arrested. Proving it was another thing, but that was starting to evolve.

Tatum was at his desk in the Identification Bureau when Julie Cooper called from Cellmark Diagnostics. Tatum braced himself for the news; The DNA banding pattern in the sperm that had been extracted from Falyssa's vagina during the autopsy matched the DNA banding pattern obtained from the vials of blood that belonged to James Rexford Powell.

A growing fourth-grader.

CHAPTER SIXTEEN

GUILTY OR NOT GUILTY

One month and two days after the crime had been committed; the Newton County District Clerk's office received a stack of paperwork from the grand jury. The top folder on the stack of cases caught the attention of District Clerk Abby Stark and her deputies.

Stark opened the folder and saw the grand jury's decision: true billed. She issued a capias, officially charging James Rexford Powell with capital murder. Rex had been charged when the search and arrest warrant was issued on October 8. A capias is a warrant that is used after an indictment has been handed down by a grand jury. Stark's signature made it official.

District Judge Joe Bob Golden had been judge of the First Judicial District of Texas since 1989. His district served the counties of Newton, Jasper, Sabine, and San Augustine. His twenty-eight years of practicing law qualified him to hold this important position of responsibility. He presided over felony criminal trials and heard testimony in civil cases and in domestic proceedings including divorces, adoptions, juveniles, and child custody battles.

Judge Golden asked Rex if he'd hired an attorney.

"No, sir," replied Rex. He did not have the money to hire an attorney, nor the means of raising funds for legal counsel. Judge Golden reminded the suspect of his rights and advised Rex that he'd appoint an attorney to represent him.

The judge knew that if Rex was found guilty and sentenced to death he would have an automatic appeal before the justices of the Texas Court of Criminal Appeals. He did not want Rex to appeal on the basis of incompetent counsel. He wanted Rex to have a seasoned defense attorney who could provide the best possible defense and who practiced law near Newton County. As the judge reviewed his list of defense attorneys, one man stood out as one of the best -- Louis Dugas of Orange County. Always willing to take on a challenge, Dugas accepted the appointment.

The single most damaging piece of evidence to Rex Powell was the DNA match up, so it was the first target in Louis Dugas' sights. If he could get Judge Golden to rule that the search warrant used to obtain blood from Rex had been obtained improperly, it would take away the most damaging evidence that the State had to offer against his client.

Court convened at the Newton County Courthouse on March 28, 1991, to hear defendant's motion to suppress the search warrant of October 8, 1990.

McWilliams called his only witness, Lt. Frank Coffin with the Beaumont Police Department. Coffin described the writing of the search and arrest warrant affidavit, the issuance of the search and arrest warrant by Judge Gist, and the execution of the warrants during the early morning hours of October 8. Coffin was excused, and legal arguments were presented.

Dugas argued that even though Judge Gist was a State District Judge, his jurisdiction included only Jefferson County. Dugas contended that Judge Gist did not have the authority to issue a search warrant to be served in Orange County (outside Jefferson County), and that the search warrant should be declared void.

"State district judges in the state of Texas have statewide authority," McWilliams said. "Judge Gist, as well as you, Judge Golden, can sit anywhere in this state and you have the power and authority to do that." Dugas argued his point to Judge Golden one last time, and the hearing was over.

Days later, McWilliams and Davis received a letter from Judge Golden. He allowed the search warrant to remain as evidence. The defendant's motion to suppress the search warrant and everything obtained from it was denied.

One of the toughest, yet most important tasks in any trial is selecting twelve people who will sit in judgment of the accused.

As jury selection officially got underway the second week in May -- seven months after Falyssa's murder -- workers in the Newton County Courthouse saw more people come through their doors than many could ever remember. More than half of the three-hundred people who had received jury summons had bona fide excuses why they could not serve. Many asked to be excused because of their ages. Some were mothers with small children at home.

When all the excuses had been heard, one-hundred-fourteen potential jurors remained. As required for capital cases, everyone received a seven page questionnaire to complete and return.

For three weeks Paul McWilliams, Charles Mitchell, Louis Dugas, and Ben Baker, a private attorney assisting Dugas, questioned the potential jurors individually. The process was slow, and even monotonous at times. But as Charles Mitchell would later remark, "You just don't pick twelve people willing to put someone to death in a couple of days."

Nine men and three women were finally seated to decide the fate of James Rexford Powell. They ranged in age from twenty-one to sixty-four. Their occupations ranged from professional, secretary, nurse, laborer, to retiree. Every one of them was a concerned, dedicated resident of Newton County. Each raised his or her right hand and swore to render a fair and impartial verdict based on the testimony and evidence presented during the trial.

The approaching weekend was Memorial Day weekend. Judge Golden set testimony to begin at 9:00 a.m., Tuesday.

As thousands of people headed to Texas lakes and beaches to welcome the beginning of summer, attorneys and investigators were making sure all of their witnesses were ready to testify.

Everyone stood as Judge Golden entered the courtroom and took his seat on the first day of trial. With a D.P.S. trooper sitting inside the north door and a game warden sitting inside the south door, the judge instructed the bailiff to bring in the jury. Falyssa's mother, Elaine Langley, silently walked to the front and took a seat. Judge Golden began:

> "Ladies and gentlemen of the jury, let me give you, briefly, some instructions again. You have been instructed not to read newspaper accounts and not to watch this on television nor listen to other people discuss this case. You also shall not discuss this case among yourselves until it comes time to deliberate. In other words, if two or three of you are together, do not discuss the evidence in the case, what you've heard or anything like that because you cannot do that until you are all together in the deliberation stage of the trial, okay? In other words, I don't want you discussing among yourselves anything about the case until it comes time to deliberate after you've heard all the evidence and the argument of counsel. I think we have a very conscientious jury. We'll try our best to conduct this trial as conveniently as possible. Will the defendant please stand?"

The Newton County District Attorney read the indictment again Rex Powell charging him with the capital murder of Falyssa Van Winkle. "James Rexford Powell, how do you plead to that indictment?" the Judge said.

"Not guilty," Rex responded matter-of-factly. It was time for opening statements.

McWilliams, in a blue pin-striped suit, starched white shirt, and blue print tie, rose to his feet. His Texas Panhandle drawl was unmistakable, but so was the serious tone in his voice as he turned to address the jury:

> "This trial is about a parent's worst nightmare. Pay close attention

to what you hear from this (witness) stand over the next two or three days and you will reach an inescapable conclusion. The only question you are to determine at this phase of the trial is, did that man right over there (pointing to Rex) do what Mr. Mitchell just read (in the indictment)? You'll know what the answer to that is once you've heard that testimony. Thank you."

Dugas reserved opening statements until the defense portion of the case.

Joe Langley was the prosecution's first witness. Through a series of questions and answers, Falyssa's step-dad testified to the events of October 6, 1990, ending with Falyssa's disappearance. McWilliams finished and passed the witness to the defense. Dugas had no questions and Joe stepped down.

The State's next witness, Judy Allen of Orange, placed Rex Powell's one-of-a-kind motor home at Larry's Antique Mall on October 6, 1990. Again, Dugas had no questions.

Next, Mitchell called Mrs. Charlie Court of Newton, a dealer at the antique mall. She stated that she saw Rex Powell beyond the peanut stand at about 10:00 a.m.

Now it was time for the prosecution witnesses to put Rex Powell in the vicinity of Cow Creek Bridge at about the time Falyssa's body was discovered.

Charles Mitchell called William Aycock of Bon Wier. Aycock described how he, Tammy Smith, and Richard Moe were playing horseshoes between 12:00 and 1:00 p.m. when a motor home passed. The witness identified Rex's motor home from photographs as the same motor home he saw going north on the dirt road.

Next came Louis Thompson. Thompson had been with his uncles Elmer and Albert Hopkins in the pickup truck that had barely collided with a motor home on the south side of Cow Creek Bridge.

Thompson's uncles related everything they saw that day, but their nephew, who is deaf, remembered seeing much more. His inability to hear sharpened his visual recollections -- another blessing for the prosecution.

Through his interpreter, Barbara Johnson, Thompson said that just as the trio passed the east end of the bridge, the white motor home with the red stripes and big red bird suddenly came up the road embankment into their lane. He was the driver, a white male, and noted that the windows had blue flowered curtains. When Thompson saw photos of the left side and the back of the motor home he confirmed it was definitely the same one that had almost collided with them that October day at Cow Creek Bridge.

Everyone watched and listened intently, witnessing a rare moment in courtroom drama as the young deaf man gave his testimony. Dugas' cross-examination of Thompson was brief, and the witness and his interpreter stepped down from the witness stand.

McWilliams called David Cassalias, who with his wife had discovered Falyssa's body under the bridge. David's testimony allowed the photograph of Falyssa's body lying face down in the muddy water to be introduced into evidence. McWilliams' next witness was D.P.S. Trooper Raleigh 'R.D.' Cox. He described following David to the bridge and finding Falyssa's body.

Pathologist Dr. Thomas Molina took the stand that afternoon. McWilliams first had him explain the reasons for autopsy and the gathering of physical evidence. Through Dr. Molina's testimony, McWilliams was able to introduce photographs taken of Falyssa's neck with the rope around it, her tied hands, her left leg, her right leg, and her bloated face.

Questioning then focused on the sexual assault examination kit and its contents. All of the evidence that had been obtained through the sexual examination was entered into evidence. These items included pulled and clipped samples of Falyssa's head hair; cotton swabs that Dr. Molina had used to swab Falyssa's vaginal area, her mouth, and her anal area; a vial of her blood; and the extra swab of the unknown substance on Falyssa's left leg. Dr. Molina's testimony also told of the vaginal focal laceration that he observed, indicating to him that a sexual assault had occurred. "There was absence of the integrity of the hymen," the doctor explained.

Dr. Molina then told of finding a bruise on Falyssa's head that was consistent with a blow with a blunt object that was probably cushioned.

Before he stepped down, the pathologist answered one last question: "Would the presence of sperm on one of the swabs that you took from the body of this little girl confirm that she was sexually assaulted?" Molina said, "Yes, of course." Ben Baker's cross-examination focused on the lack of bruising, blood or exterior laceration in Falyssa's genital area.

McWilliams' next witness for the afternoon was Newton County Sheriff's Deputy Ricky Hillin. He introduced the piece of white cotton rope found in a bush close to Falyssa's body.

Next came Deputy Curtis Whittaker. Through his testimony, McWilliams continued to show the chain of custody as Whittaker told how he recovered the hair band found near Falyssa's body. He then testified how he later turned over the hair band and the rope to Boyd Lamb with the Beaumont Police Department.

Justice of the Peace A.J. Satterwhite was the next witness for the state. The judge testified about holding auctions at his general store on Saturday nights and how he recalled seeing Rex Powell on the afternoon of October 6, 1990. He also testified Rex arrived at his store between 3:45 and 4:30 p.m., visited for a few minutes, then drove away.

The state's next witness was twelve-year-old Shannon Kirk, who lived across the street from Rex. Sheriff Powell had visited with the young witness and his friend Jared Stidham, who lived next door to the defendant, a couple weeks after the investigation began. Shannon described how he and Jared were playing football in Jared's front yard about 4:00 or 5:00 p.m. Sunday afternoon October 7 when they saw Mr. Powell washing his motor home thoroughly inside and outside. He also testified that Rex carried several boxes out of the vehicle.

Wednesday morning's testimony began with Sheriff Wayne Powell. Mitchell used Sheriff Powell's testimony to clarify the route Louis Thompson, Elmer, and Albert would have traveled coming back from their shopping trip in Kirbyville to their home in the Newton County community of Sand Jack. Dugas' cross-examination became mired in confusion and ended quickly.

Identification technician Sue Kelly's testimony dealt with her attendance at Falyssa'a autopsy, supporting the important chain of custody of evidence.

Frank Coffin took the stand and answered questions about Rex and his motor home. Coffin told the jury about serving the arrest and search warrant on Rex Powell. McWilliams showed Coffin photographs of the motor home, and he identified it as the one confiscated from Rex. Coffin then told how Rex was taken to Baptist Hospital in Beaumont, where four vials of blood were taken.

As Coffin continued his testimony, the envelope, state's exhibit number 31, and the four vials of blood, marked state's exhibits 31-A, 31-B, 31-C, and 31-D were introduced into the court record. The police officer concluded his testimony by telling how he had delivered the envelope and its contents to Julie Cooper at the Cellmark Laboratory in Germantown, Maryland.

McWilliams continued his chain of custody testimony concerning the vital evidence that had been entered into the court record. Witness Bill Tatum told how the seized evidence was turned over to him as it was collected. He stated that he delivered the samples of hair and ropes to Agent Doug Deedrick at the F.B.I Laboratory in Washington, D.C.

Through Tatum's testimony, McWilliams introduced into evidence photographs of the motor home's damaged air conditioner cowling as well as photographs of the underside of Cow Creek Bridge. Tatum told about the discovery of the damaged air conditioner cowling as the vehicle was being inspected at the police department. He told about discovering the scrape on the underside of the bridge and how the height of the motor home appeared to be approximately the same as the height from the underside of the bridge to the ground.

Pitifully, Dugas' cross-examination tried to show that Tatum had deflated the tires to get it under the bridge. Tatum explained that he drove the motor home with the same amount of tire pressure that had been in the tires when the vehicle was seized.

Doug Deedrick introduced himself to the jury and explained his qualifications as a Special Agent of the Federal Bureau of Investigation. He gave jurors a short course in hair and fiber analysis, then McWilliams began to zero in on the hair evidence. He showed Deedrick the state's exhibits and asked if any of Falyssa's hairs were found inside the motor home. Deedrick said, "Yes."

McWilliams then asked about any unusual characteristics of the hairs Deedrick had determined belonging to Falyssa. He restated that all of the questioned hairs that had been recovered from under the plywood splinter on the floor of the defendant's motor home had been forcibly removed from Falyssa's scalp.

Agent Deedrick testified that the rope found in the bushes close to Falyssa's body matched the ropes that were found around her neck and wrists. He stated the ropes confiscated from Rex's motor home were not the same type rope as the type found on the child's body and in the bush under the bridge.

Dugas tried to discredit Deedrick but the agent's testimony was solid.

With the DNA testing, McWilliams knew that he was dealing

with a highly complicated and scientific subject. He also knew that a picture was worth a thousand words, so when Julie Cooper of Cellmark took the stand, she brought a chart to help explain the complex subject a little more easily.

Cooper said, "There is an 11-step procedure which we call DNA Profiling, which we follow in the laboratory to enable us to remove or extract the DNA from the cells and break it up and create what's called a DNA banding pattern. And it's this DNA banding pattern that we look at, analyze, and we know what your individual allegedly looks like from this DNA banding pattern."

McWilliams had done his homework. He let his questions lead Cooper into explaining a complex scientific test in terms that the jury, and everyone in the courtroom, could understand.

McWilliams then questioned Cooper about Cellmark's internal checks to make sure no mistakes had been made through this detailed series of tests.

Back to the case at hand, Cooper was asked how DNA from the vaginal swab of Falyssa Van Winkle compared to DNA extracted from Rex's blood.

Cooper identified the DNA banding pattern that had come from Rex Powell's blood. She showed to the jury the DNA banding pattern that had come from the sperm that had been removed on the swab during Falyssa's sexual assault examination. It matched the DNA banding pattern of Rex Powell.

In classic defense style, Louis Dugas attacked Julie Cooper, her company, the procedures used to conduct the tests, and everything else that came to his mind. But Cooper was an exceptional witness, an expert in her field, and seasoned veteran on the witness stand. Dugas couldn't shake her confidence.

McWilliams called Dr. Dan Garner, Director of Laboratories for

Cellmark Diagnostics, to show that Cooper had followed proper protocol in her tests of the evidence.

The chief prosecutor then called his last witness, Elaine Langley. All eyes were on Falyssa's mother as she slowly walked to the witness stand and sat down.

"On October 6, 1990, did you give Falyssa permission to leave Larry's Antique Mall with anybody?" McWilliams said. Elaine said she did not.

Elaine was shown the photo of her dead little girl, taken while Falyssa was still lying in the mud puddle under the bridge, with the ropes still around her neck and wrists. McWilliams asked her if that was Falyssa's body. Fighting back tears and with a quiver in her voice, her answer was simple, "Yes, it is."

Dugas evidently did not want to antagonize the jury. "No questions," he stated.

As the state's case closed, McWilliams was confident that he and Mitchell had proven, not only beyond a reasonable doubt, as the law required, but beyond any doubt, that James Rexford Powell had abducted, raped, and murdered Falyssa Van Winkle.

Dugas had not given an opening statement at the beginning of the trial; he had reserved that right for the beginning of his defense.

Dugas called his first witness, Handley Jones. Everybody close to the investigation was shocked. Handley Jones? Was this all the defense had to offer? The state knew all about Handley Jones, a man who had been stopped a month after the killing for a traffic violation in Newton. He remarked to the officer that the wrong man was locked up for killing the little girl. The officer had relayed the information to Sheriff Powell who had passed the information on to Davis and Tatum.

Handley hadn't wanted to talk to the detectives at first, but Davis had told him he could be the key to setting an innocent man free. Jones had said he had a flat tire about 2:00 p.m. Saturday, October 6 next to the creek bridge. His spare was also flat and he tried to flag a red van that had driven under the creek bridge. He said the red van and its driver stayed under the bridge for about ten minutes, then drove out from under the bridge back onto Hwy. 1416 the way it had come. Handley told the detectives if they found the driver of the red van they'd find the girl's killer.

Davis was skeptical. He asked Jones what time he had left his house that day. "About noon, I guess," the man had said. They calculated the time Jones took to drive to the bridge, get help to fix the flat, and drive away. Instead of being at the bridge at 2:00 to 2:30 p.m., it appeared that Jones was at the bridge nearer 1:00 to 1:30 p.m. Davis and Tatum knew from talking to other witnesses exactly where Rex Powell was with Falyssa's dead body at that time. Davis recalled their visit to the unlikely witness and this testimony for the grand jury. For the defense of capital murder, the testimony of Handley Jones was almost laughable.

On the witness stand, Dugas had Jones tell his story. Jones stated he saw the driver of the red van, and that person was definitely *not* Rex Powell.

McWilliams began his cross-examination. He asked Jones how he knew that the Saturday he had the flat was October 6. "How do we know it wasn't the Saturday before or the Saturday after?" McWilliams asked.

Frustrated, Jones responded, "Well, it just wasn't." McWilliams had also caught on to the fact that while Mr. Jones and Dugas had talked about the bridge, they had never specifically mentioned that Jones had his flat at Cow Creek Bridge.

McWilliams had Jones retrace his route from his house to the bridge, describing every turn. Jones got so frustrated at one point that he asked Judge Golden to recess the trial to take everyone to the bridge he was talking about. The judge declined. McWilliams had to remind Jones of the conversation he'd had with Detective Davis to make sure his story from November 8 and his story on the witness stand were the same. Jones admitted that the red van he'd seen go under the bridge could have gone under there for many reasons. McWilliams had not had to discredit Jones' testimony. He'd just shown it had nothing to do with Falyssa's murder. Dugas didn't have any more questions for Jones, and the man gladly stepped down.

"Next witness?" Judge Golden asked Dugas.

"We rest," the defense attorney replied. McWilliams and Mitchell looked at the defense attorneys in disbelief. Where were all of the expert witnesses to refute the state's expert witnesses? Where were all of the alibi witnesses for Rex saying he and his motor home were somewhere else that Saturday afternoon in October, other than under Cow Creek Bridge disposing of Falyssa's body? Maybe it was because the expert testimony couldn't be refuted. Maybe it was because there were no alibi witnesses.

On June 3, final arguments began. Judge Golden reminded the jurors that the arguments were *not* evidence, and that to reach their verdict jurors had to rely on the testimony from the witness stand. Because the state had the burden of proof, prosecutors get to argue first and last, with the defense in between. Mitchell went first and recounted how witnesses and evidence affirmatively placed Rex with Falyssa on that fateful day, in that one-of-a-kind motor home. Mitchell then showed the jury the rope that had been taken from Falyssa's neck. He glared and pointed at Rex. Mitchell ended his argument by reminding the jurors of all of the evidence that had been brought forth and analyzed in this case and about the testimony of the prosecution medical and scientific experts.

"Please don't let this guy get away with this. I urge you to find him guilty, because he *is* guilty. *There is no presumption of innocence any longer; we've met our burden*," Mitchell emphasized.

Defense Attorney Ben Baker went first for their team. He agreed that the death of this little girl was a terrible crime. Then he began attacking the credibility of nearly all of the state's witnesses. His argument also tried to insinuate that the detectives investigating the child's murder had manipulated some of the evidence so that it would point more in the direction of Rex Powell than in the direction of the actual killer. But the final portion of Baker's argument might have incited the jury rather than swayed them in the defense's direction.

"The bottom line is, that girl wasn't raped," he said. "There were some signs there but there was no hemorrhaging from the girl's hymen, there were no bruises or lacerations or cuts on her legs, and, folks, she was fully clothed." Falyssa's family and the investigators were shocked at this argument, but tried to stay calm as the defense attorney continued.

Baker then attacked Agent Deedrick's testimony along with the testimony of Julie Cooper and Dr. Garner. In closing, he said, "We want to hate somebody for this, but, folks, if we're going to hate somebody let's be sure we hate the right man. I think the evidence in this case dictates that the only verdict this jury can render is not guilty."

Louis Dugas is considered one of the best criminal defense attorneys in the state and he pulled out all the stops in his final moments with the jury. Experienced courtroom observers noted that he did the best he could with what he had in the case, which was not much.

Dugas attacked the credibility of the state's witnesses and questioned why some other potential state's witnesses weren't called to testify. He was trying everything in his power to create that element of doubt in the mind of just one juror. Then he went for the jury's emotions.

"You must ask yourself -- can you, in your day-to-day affairs, week-to-week, month-to-month, in the morning when you fix your hair, when you shave, look yourself in the eye and say, 'I did the right thing?' If you have reasonable doubt, you must vote not guilty... I ask you to go in and after you've deliberated and after you've talked and after you've talked again, I ask that you find Rex Powell not guilty."

After the defense concluded, Paul McWilliams eagerly stepped to the podium to respond to certain arguments that had outraged the prosecutors.

"The thing that I want to address, because I guess it's the thing that raises my hackles quicker than anything, is Mr. Baker's comment about fabrication. I told most of you on jury selection, there's no secret about being a juror. It just takes people with common sense. Well, does it make sense to you good people that the Jefferson County District Attorney's Office, the Newton County District Attorney's Office, the Newton County Sheriff's Office, the Orange County Sheriff's Office, the Beaumont Police Department, the FBI, and everybody concerned would need to lie, cheat, and steal so we can convict the wrong man to insure that there is a child killer still out there? Ben Baker doesn't buy that, and you folks don't buy that either."

McWilliams then turned to the defense's argument that Falyssa was not *raped* in the course of her murder. McWilliams could hardly control his anger as he pointed to Rex and said:

"Are they saying that ten-year-old Falyssa Van Winkle consensually had sex with that man right there? That's kind of what it sounded like."

McWilliams then explained to the jury why certain actions were taken during the investigation and why certain witnesses had been called to testify and not others. The defense had muddied the water and McWilliams wanted to clear it up. He also addressed the statistical evidence from the DNA experts.

"Probably one of the biggest debates here is that one-in-two-million number. Dan Garner told you where those numbers came from. They know how many people have a certain ban frequency. Dan Garner told you that although eight (DNA) bands showed up, they just used seven to calculate the one-in-two-million. One of them, it matched, but it was below their marker range. Dr. Garner obviously knew what he was talking about. They told you there are times when they literally give a suspect the benefit of the doubt. You'll remember that Mr. Dugas asked Dan Garner out of the population of the United States, (one-in-two-million) that means one-hundred-twenty-five people and you don't have any indication that all of those people don't live right here in Newton County. So, let's assume that all one-hundred-twenty-five of those folks that had that (DNA) banding pattern live right here in Newton County."

It seemed a far-fetched tangent but so did many of the defense arguments. McWilliams proceeded,

"How many of those people can contribute DNA from sperm? Well, let's figure half of them. Half of them men, half of them women, and we'll give the benefit of the doubt, we'll say sixty-three men. Well, of those men, how many of them went to Larry's (Antique Mall) that day? Okay, maybe half again, thirty-two. How many of them went to Larry's that morning? Well, let's give them the benefit of the doubt again, we'll just say half, so we're at sixteen. How many of them left Larry's Antique Mall that morning? Let's say half again, eight. How many of them knew Falyssa Van Winkle well enough to get close to her, to get her into a motor home without causing a scene out there with a bunch of people? Let's give them the benefit of the doubt again, let's say half again. So we've got four folks. How many of them were back driving around in Newton County that afternoon? Well, let say that two of those, we'll give them that half again, that two of these folks were."

McWilliam zeroed in on his target.

"And how many of them were driving that motor home? Well,

we're kind of down to one, aren't we?"

McWilliams thrust his finger at Rex and for a few seconds, a powerful silence enveloped the courtroom. The jury went into deliberate. It was 11:30 a.m.

Even seasoned lawyers and judges are reluctant to guess how long a jury will deliberate in a capital murder case. Everyone can think of extremes on each end of the spectrum, from less than an hour to more than a week. On that day in Newton County, virtually everyone involved thought the jury would take their lunch break and then deliberate in the afternoon. Several prosecution witnesses left for a quick lunch so they could be back before the jury *began* their deliberation.

At 12:15 p.m. there was a buzz in the hallway outside the courtroom as someone yelled that the jury had reached a verdict. It seemed impossible, as final arguments had concluded only forty-five minutes earlier. As the interested parties tried to determine if this was a courthouse prank, the Judge re-convened the trial for the reading of the verdict. As is normal in emotionally-charged cases, Judge Golden strongly admonished everyone in the standing-room-only courtroom to give no reaction whatsoever, no matter what the verdict. All eyes were on the twelve jurors as they walked single-file into the courtroom and took their seats in the jury box.

Judge Golden observed the formalities by silently viewing the jury form before asking District Clerk Abbie Start to read it aloud. While many people in the courtroom held their breath, the clerk read, "We the jury, find the defendant, James Rexford Powell, *guilty* of capital murder."

At nine o'clock that morning, Rex Powell had entered the courtroom an innocent man in the eyes of the law. He sat with no expression as the verdict was read. He stood with no expression when the jury declared him guilty of capital murder. He showed no expression as he was handcuffed and led to the door of the courtroom. Less than four hours after Rex Powell entered the courtroom that morning, he exited the same door as a man convicted of the kidnapping, rape, and death of a ten-year-old girl. And the ordeal was not over.

The stately Newton County Courthouse, one of the first
grand-style courthouses built in Texas.

Cow Creek Bridge where Rex Powell drove onto
Hwy. 1416 into the path of Lewis Thompson,
and Elmer and Albert Hopkins.

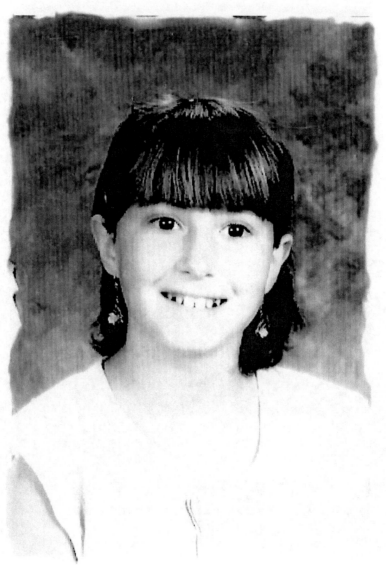

A young lady, almost ten years old.

CHAPTER SEVENTEEN

LIFE OR DEATH

Having found Rex Powell guilty of capital murder, the jury's only remaining task was to assess punishment. In Texas, jurors do this indirectly by answering specific questions about the defendant's continuing danger to society. Depending on the jury's answers, the Judge assesses either life in prison or death by lethal injection.

McWilliams' first witness in the punishment phase was a woman Rex thought he had defeated for good almost seven years before, Lucille Jackson. As expected, Dugas immediately objected, arguing Rex had been found not guilty in the 1985 Louisiana trial, and that her testimony amounted to trying Rex twice for the same crime. McWilliams countered that Rex's involvement in the 1984 incident was relevant and admissible in the punishment phase. Judge Golden overruled the objection, clearing the way for the seventy-three year-old woman to have her day in court -- again.

With the embodiment of grandmotherly affection, Jackson told the jury of the horrific events of August 2, 1984. At the end of McWilliams' direct examination, Jackson again identified Rex as the man who had tried to rape and kill her.

Next came Bruce Quave, who again testified to seeing Rex, sporting a full beard, in the yellow Jeep just before Jackson was attacked. Quave told of seeing Rex just after the time of the attack, having shaved his beard, and with fresh scratch wounds on both wrists.

The next witness, Justice Neely, was in a precarious position with both sides as he took the stand. Falyssa's family considered him responsible, in part, for Rex's 1985 acquittal in the Lucille Jackson case. (See Chapter Twelve for his 1984 testimony.) Because Neely was changing his controversial story, Rex Powell was not glad to see the man who would *now* place him near Lucille Jackson's home in 1984.

Prosecutors brought out that Neely recalled *two* yellow Jeeps in 1984, and that Rex Powell was driving one of them. Neely also admitted to the Newton County jury that he had made Rex's bond in 1984 and that this fact had not been disclosed to the Beauregard Parish jury. Dugas tried to impeach Neely on the two seemingly inconsistent statements, but Neely would not waver from his identification of Rex. Some courtroom observers were sympathetic to the elderly Neely during his subdued and remorseful testimony. Others thought he was little better than Rex, but gave him some credit for testifying truthfully in Falyssa's trial.

Mitchell called the state's last two witnesses: Louis Cooper, Merryville's former Chief of Police, and Robert McCullough, Beauregard Parish Sheriff's Deputy. Both men testified that they had known Rex for a number of years, and that for all his self-glorification, the "Mayor of Mauriceville" had a reputation in the community that was bad -- all bad.

Prosecutors then rested, believing they had presented more than enough evidence for the jury to answer the critical questions which would guarantee the death penalty.

Dugas called Merryville resident William Thompson to the witness stand. Thompson stated that he didn't think Rex would be violent. Under cross-examination, McWilliams showed the elderly man the photo of Falyssa's body. "Would you think that somebody that would do that to a ten-year-old girl is capable of violence?" McWilliams asked.

Thompson's response was undeniable -- "Yes."

Next up for the defense was Rex's wife. Baker tried to appeal to jurors' emotions as Corliss gave a biographical sketch of Rex's life. She described Rex as a husband, as a father, and as a hard-working person. "He wouldn't have any inclination for criminal acts of violence," Corliss said.

"You would have said that about Rex before October 6, 1990, wouldn't you?" McWilliams asked as he began his cross-examination. "Yes, I would," Corliss responded.

"You would have said that before August 2, 1984, wouldn't you?" McWilliams asked, "Oh, yes," Corliss said.

When McWilliams revealed past accusations concerning Rex's sexual conduct with his niece, Cindy, and their daughter, Nancy, Corliss quickly denied there had been any problems with either girl. Again, McWilliams showed the photo of Falyssa with the rope around her neck. "Whoever did this is pretty mean, aren't they?" he asked.

"Very possibly," Corliss admitted.

Witness testimony for the punishment phase of the trial was over. When court reconvened, Judge Golden again read the charge to the jury and attorneys stepped forward for final arguments.

In his final plea to jurors, prosecutor Mitchell made a key point that hit home.

"He hasn't done it once; he's done it twice. You folks are the jury, but you're more than a jury. *You are the only thing between him and the next victim.*"

Dugas began his final remarks by paraphrasing several Bible stories. He asked the jury to spare Rex's life. He talked about the history of the death penalty in Texas. Then he picked up a brown paper bag, and walked to the jury box. He removed the contents of the bag and held them up for everyone to see.

"I have here twelve syringes; one for each of you. Could you inject the poison yourself? Could you do this? You're doing it by proxy when you say, "yes." So, I ask you that when you retire to vote on this, that your answer be "no.""

He sat down, leaving the syringes behind on the desk. Prosecutors had seen this ploy numerous times and were not impressed.

Again, Baker appealed to the jurors' sense of responsibility -- and conscience.

"Remember that just as Rex Powell is going to live with his decision, you are going to have to live with your decision."

With the grisly details of the crime foremost in his thinking, McWilliams punctuated his case like a hell-fire and brimstone preacher.

"I think you know why he did what he did to Falyssa. There were two things that he wanted from her. Some of you may have thought there was just one, and that he accomplished that one thing, and the accomplishment of that is ultimately what led to his conviction because he left the evidence."

McWilliams' voice grew louder and he pointed out Rex's real motivation for the crime:

"But the other thing that James Rexford Powell wanted was the power, the feeling of control that he has when he's got a ten-year-old down flat on her back in the back of that motor home and he can do anything he wants with her. *That's* his high. *That's* what drives him. *That's* what makes him tick. And you can just almost picture, as he draws that cord tighter and tighter, the good feeling he gets from that. And that terrifies good people like us."

For perhaps the last time, McWilliams held up the photo of the ligature intact.

"This is a hard picture to look at but it is Rex Powell's handiwork. And as Charles Mitchell told you, he's proud of it. He left it there. He left it there for people to see because he doesn't think he is touchable. He doesn't think you folks will get him. And now we know why, don't we, when we heard the story from Lucille Jackson. It's time for you to tell Rex Powell and those like him, 'Never again, never again.' I will do my part, I will do what my oath requires me to say, Rex Powell, never again, *never again*, will you have an opportunity to get close to anybody and rob them of the rest of their lives. I don't care how bad you want that feeling of power. I don't care how bad you want to have sex with a ten-year-old; I'm going to stop it. The twelve of us are going to stop it so that it never, never, never happens again."

Those in the courtroom remember the bold and effective way McWilliams ended his argument.

"The law in clear; the evidence is clear. You do your duty, then the judge will do his and sentence this man to death. Rex Powell wrote his own death warrant. He wrote it in the sand under Cow Creek Bridge. He wrote it with those ropes. Now it's time for you folks to serve that warrant on him. Because none of you, *none of you*, want the situation where we've got to bring Elaine Langley and Michael Van Winkle into a courtroom, along with Lucille Jackson *again,* and say, well, let us tell you what happened several years ago. *Never again. "*

Everyone in the standing-room-only courtroom had clung to his every word.

Judge Golden retired the jury, and the court was recessed for the last time. Some of the people stayed in the courtroom. Others left and walked outside or mingled in the corridors. No one dared venture far. They knew how quickly the jury had convicted Rex of his crimes; many were betting that this time, they wouldn't take that long.

Bill Davis was sipping coffee in the district clerk's office, when Dugas walked in and poured himself a cup. The two men who had been on opposite ends of the trial stood side by side.

"I'm glad you were appointed to represent Rex," Davis said. Warily, the defense attorney looked at the detective. Dugas thanked him for the compliment, then asked, "Why?" "Because I wanted Rex to have the best," Davis explained, adding, "I wanted our facts and our evidence to go up against the best, and I didn't want Rex to have any issue on appeal of incompetent counsel." Dugas's smiling response was a tribute to each and every person who had participated in the investigation. He said, "It's hard to climb out of a hole when you can't even make it to the first rung of the ladder."

Word of the jury's return spread like a grass fire in a high wind throughout the courthouse. The twelve Newton County residents had deliberated for a little more than half an hour.

Sheriff Powell was sitting on the front row directly behind Rex when Davis and Tatum entered the courtroom. "After sentencing, I want the three of us to escort Rex back to the jail," Powell said to Davis and Tatum.

"No, Wayne, that's a job and privilege for you and your deputies," Tatum said.

True to form, the sheriff was unshakable. "The two of you did most of the investigation, and deserve the honor of walking him out of here." The two Beaumont lawmen knew it was useless to argue. They were honored by Powell's comments.

With the jury still outside the courtroom, Judge Golden reconvened, then turned to the standing-room-only audience.

"Ladies and gentlemen, I understand there is a verdict in the case. No matter what the verdict, I don't want anything said or any demonstrations in the courtroom. I'm going to ask everyone to stay in their seats, exactly where you are, including the jury, until the defendant is out of the courtroom."

The judge noded and the bailiff escorted the jurors to their seats. The jury foreperson handed the papers to the judge. As he had done with the first verdict, Judge Golden reviewed it, and then nodded for the verdict to be read.

"We, the jury, unanimously find and determine beyond a reasonable doubt that the answer to Special Issue #1 is, "Yes." "We, the jury, unanimously find and determine beyond a reasonable doubt that the answer to Special Issue #2 is, "Yes."

Judge Golden turned back to the jury. "I'm going to call the name of each and every juror and poll you, which means I want you to answer, 'Yes,' if this is your verdict."

As each juror's name was called, he or she stood, looked directly at Rex, and said, "Yes," emphatically. *Yes, Rex Powell killed Falyssa. Yes, he is a danger to society. And yes, he must die for his crime.*

Without a smile, without a tear, the "Mayor of Mauriceville" rose to his feet along with his attorneys.

Looking directly at Rex, Judge Golden stated, "James Rexford Powell, pursuant to the mandatory provisions of Article 37.071 of the Code of Criminal Procedure, I assess your punishment at death."

The judge asked Sheriff Powell to remove the defendant. Powell approached Rex with Tatum and Davis at his side. The three lawmen escorted the condemned killer out the west door of the courtroom. They stopped in the corridor and Davis handcuffed the prisoner. It was the second and last time Bill Davis handcuffed the man from Mauriceville.

As they descended the steep stairway to the main level of the courthouse, Rex spoke. Powell held Rex's left arm, Davis held Rex's right arm, and Tatum followed directly behind the killer. "Could you go a little slower?" Rex asked. "I have a bad leg."

A minute later Rex was back in his cell at the Newton County Jail awaiting transfer to Death Row at the state prison in Huntsville. The courtroom was quiet and somber. There were neither cheers of joy nor tears of anguish. Prosecutors were accepting congratulations from a stream of supporters.

Elaine remained seated as a procession of people shook her hand, hugged her neck, or simply whispered, "God Bless You." Clutching a red rose, her response was a bittersweet "thank you." It came from her heart, and from her daughter's.

The Newton County courtroom where James Rexford Powell was sentenced to death.

CHAPTER EIGHTEEN

SINCE THE TRIAL...

Having received the death penalty, by law Rex was given an automatic appeal to the Texas Court of Criminal Appeals. Louis Dugas continued to represent Rex through the automatic appeal.

Dugas's main points of appeal were an objection to results of DNA testing being allowed into testimony to the jury under conditional circumstances, and an objection to evidence from Ms. Jackson's case being allowed into testimony during the punishment phase of the trial, since Rex had been acquitted in Louisiana.

On June 14, 1995, the Texas Court of Criminal Appeals rejected Dugas' arguments and affirmed Rex's conviction and punishment.

With the 1995 affirmation by the higher court, Dugas had fulfilled his legal obligation to Rex and to the judicial system. Rex needed a new attorney to represent him with other appeals and legal maneuvers available through the judicial process. The Texas Court of Criminal Appeals appointed David Bays of San Antonio. Bays filed a Writ of Habeas Corpus for Rex shortly after the court's 1995 ruling. On April 1, 1998, Rex's Writ of Habeas Corpus was denied. All of Rex's appeals through the state courts were now exhausted.

In April 1998, Bays stated in a telephone conversation with Sgt. Davis, that he would file federal appeals in Beaumont. He said, "Under new laws passed to expedite the process, Rex's federal appeals should be completed within nine months to a year. When all appeals have been exhausted, Judge Joe Bob Golden will carry out the Newton County jury's decision of punishment and issue a death warrant for Rex."

While Bays maneuverd through the federal judicial appellate process, Rex had a new place of residence. He was TDCJ Inmate #1999001, housed at the Texas Department of Criminal Justice-Ellis

Unit. Home for more than four-hundred death row inmates, the prison is twelve miles north of Huntsville in Walker County, Texas. Within the unit, Rex was housed in Cellblock H17, allocated for death row inmates who have a 'work-capable trustee' status.

Rex's day began at 7:00 a.m. He worked in the garment factory making uniforms for corrections officers. He was allowed to leave his cell and could move about freely in the exercise yard or recreation room from 7:00 a.m. to 11:00 p.m., except when he was working. He did not wear restraints unless he left the prison unit.

But during this time, Rex was alive. His appeals were being heard. He was being allowed many chances to live, to be set free, to beat the rap -- far more opportunities than those he gave to a precious little girl named Falyssa Van Winkle.

*   *   *

Lucile Jackson died January 21, 1996, at the age of seventy-eight. Her courage and spirit will live on in her daughter, Myrna Cooley and grandson, Cary.

Justice Neely died near the same time as Mrs. Jackson. His reputation is still tarnished by his 1985 testimony that helped exonerate Rex Powell in Lucille Jackson's case.

Falyssa's older sister, Shonna Van Winkle McBride, twenty-one, married and graduated at McNeese State University in Lake Charles, majoring in biology. Shonna spent eighteen months assisting a micro-biology professor with DNA research. She also applied for post-graduate programs and scholarships to pursue her Ph.D. in biology.

Falyssa Van Winkle would have celebrated her nineteenth birthday on December 14, 1998 -- two days after the publication of this book.

Christmas 1987, age eight and positively angelic.

CHAPTER NINETEEN

REX POWELL - DEAD MAN WALKING**

While Rex was working in the garment factory at the Ellis Unit awaiting the fate of his appeals, others involved in Falyssa's case were having life changing events occur in their lives.

Sheriff Wayne Powell was stricken with a massive stroke on September 11, 1998. The stroke affected his use of his left arm and leg. His speech was also severely affected. Through intense therapy, the sheriff regained his speech in a few weeks and was back to his wit and humor. Six weeks in the hospital and continued therapy helped Sheriff Powell regain partial use of his left leg. He never regained use of his left arm. Wayne's physical afflictions slowed him down, but his law enforcement experience and mental capabilities enabled him to continue being sheriff of Newton County. If you were ever down and needed a pick-me-up, you just needed to stop by Wayne's office on the first floor of the Newton County Courthouse. He was quick to profess his love for God and his quick wit and humor had you laughing in no time at all. Sheriff Wayne Powell passed away March 27, 2009. At his funeral, Bill Davis preached the service.

Bill Tatum retired from the Beaumont Police Department on January 31, 2001. He had begun his police career as a patrol officer, working the "streets." He spent time as an identification technician, as a motorcycle officer, as a detective/sergeant, and finally as the supervisor of the identification unit. His skills at crime scenes were second to none. He'd given thirty-three years of his life protecting the citizens of Beaumont and enforcing the law, but looked forward to spending time with his wife (and high school sweetheart), Brenda.

"Dead man walking" is a common prison term for an inmate on death row taking his last walk. That walk is from his cell on death row to the death chamber.

He and Brenda were going to spend a lot of time visiting with their three daughters and sons-in-law, and playing with their grandchildren.

About a month after retirement, Bill and Brenda, along with their eldest daughter, Kim, her husband, Lowell, and their three children headed to Pagosa Springs, Colorado. It was time to really enjoy retirement skiing, building snowmen, and having snowball fights with the kids and grandkids. On March 12, 2001, Bill had just finished helping the grandchildren build a snowman in front of their cabin at the beautiful ski resort. He was in his element - living life to its fullest with his beautiful wife, his daughter and son-in-law, and grandchildren, and was chasing one of his grandsons when his chest began to feel heavy. Bill suddenly fell unconscious on the snow-covered ground. Being a doctor, Lowell immediately began administering CPR. An ambulance was called and Bill was rushed to a nearby hospital. He was pronounced dead a short time later. He suffered a massive heart attack. Bill had been retired only thirty-nine days. He was a Christian, a husband, a father, a grandfather, and a mentor and friend to many. Bill Tatum is sorely missed.

Falyssa's mother and step-father, Elaine and Joe Langley moved in 2001 from Lake Charles, Louisiana, to San Antonio, Texas. Joe was able to obtain a job transfer that enabled him and Elaine to move closer to Falyssa's big sister, Shonna, who had finished school, enlisted in the military, married, and had a baby. Joe and Elaine wanted to be able to spend quality time with their family.

Bill Davis continued investigating sex crimes incidents and traveling through the United States presenting child abuse seminars and school safety programs. In October, 1998, Davis returned from speaking at the Texas CASA (Court Appointed Special Advocates) annual conference in Corpus Christi, Texas, to learn that after more than twenty years of investigating child abuse and sex crimes cases and while out of town, he had been transferred to the patrol division as a patrol supervisor. Bill had gained tremendous popularity in the community from his awareness seminars and programs. He had also spent one year in the mid-1980's presenting Crime Stoppers crimes on television every week. Bill's transfer stopped him from investigating child abuse and sex crimes investigations. But, it also gave him more freedom to proactively present programs and save even more lives. (Bill continues to be in much demand even to this day as a motivational speaker.)

Life always seems to take its toll. In 2001, Bill and his wife, Jan, separated after twenty-eight years of marriage. A divorce followed a few months later. As Bill worked the South Texas State Fair in October, 2001, he visited with many of his longtime friends he saw once a year at the ten-day event. One of these friends receiving an annual visit was American Red Cross volunteer and paramedic, Mary Justice. Bill and Mary began dating a short time later. They were married January 10, 2003. Mary manages Bill's speaking career and travels with him throughout the country.

Mike Van Winkle, Bill Davis, and others kept track of Rex's appeals as the years went by. His federal appeals process went through a federal court of original jurisdiction within the Eastern District of Texas. Rex's guilt and punishment were upheld. His case was then appealed to the 5th Circuit Court of Appeals in New Orleans, Louisiana. His guilt and punishment were upheld again. His case was then appealed to the United States Supreme Court. After reviewing the evidence, the Supreme Court justices refused to hear Rex's appeal. When Rex's appeal to the Supreme Court of the United States was denied, Judge Joe Bob Golden issued a death warrant for Rex. His execution date was set for October 1, 2002.

As Rex's execution date neared, the Texas Department of Criminal Justice began making preparations. Rex's family was allowed to have five witnesses at the execution and the victim's family was allowed to have five witnesses. The news media was also allowed to have witnesses present for the execution. Falyssa's father, Mike Van Winkle, wanted to fill the five allotted slots for the victim's family with his side of the family, including his current wife and his ex-wife that he was married to at the time of Falyssa's death. Joe and Elaine decided not to attend the execution but requested to the Texas Department of

Criminal Justice that their witness slots be filled by Bill Davis and Wayne Powell. This request was adamantly opposed by Mike Van Winkle. But in the end, the Texas Department of Criminal Justice granted Elaine's request. Bill and Wayne were going to watch Rex die in Falyssa's behalf.

The Texas Department of Criminal Justice handles more executions than any other state in the United States. All executions are handled in the death chamber at the "Walls Unit" in downtown Huntsville. A new death row cell block had been built in Livingston, Texas at the Polunsky Penitentiary Unit and Rex, along with all the other death row inmates had been transferred from the Ellis Unit to the new facility in 1999. The morning of October 1st, Rex was transported from the Polunsky Prison Unit to the "Walls" a distance of forty-three miles. His request for his last meal was a pot of coffee. Witnesses for the victim's family met at the First Baptist Church next to the prison. Witnesses for Rex met at another location about a block away. It was 1:30 p.m.

Bill Davis and his fiancee, Mary, were the first to arrive at the church. Mike Van Winkle, his wife and his sister were the next ones to arrive. Finally, Sheriff Powell arrived at the church. The sheriff had a friend drive him from Newton to Huntsville because his physical challenges made long trips difficult. Bill was glad to see his friend, but was surprised to see that he walked with such difficulty into the family witness waiting room. Handshakes were exchanged and Bill introduced his fiancee to the sheriff. As time began to draw near, Mr. Gene Stewart, TDCJ victim witness coordinator, explained each step of the execution procedure. Everyone understood all of the steps involved and knew there could be no outbursts or signs of emotion.

Small talk filled another thirty to forty-five minutes of the afternoon. A basket of fruit and snacks, soft drinks, and bottled water were provided to the guests by the membership of the church. Everyone sampled the snacks and had something to drink. Mr. Stewart looked at him watch. "It's time," he said. "We need to get to our vehicles and go to the Walls." It was 4:30 p.m.

It was suddenly here. It was time to see some meager form of justice served for the kidnapping, rape, and murder of an innocent ten-year-old little girl.

Everyone got into their respective vehicles. Mary left in Bill's truck to spend the next hour-and-a-half touring the prison system's new museum and driving Huntsville's streets. Bill rode with Mr. Stewart. The defunct prison rodeo arena came into view as they drove around the backside of the "Walls." Mr. Stewart explained that the once popular prison rodeos ended when the arena structure became too old and unstable to support the standing-room-only crowds several years ago. The vehicles parked in the main parking lot in front of the main entrance to the "Walls." Bill helped Wayne escalate the steps to the front door. Everyone produced a photo I.D. and gave it to a TDJC guard just inside the front door. Steel bars with a locked steel bar door prohibited everyone from going further into the building. Mr. Stewart asked the guard to acquire a wheelchair for Sheriff Powell. While waiting for the wheelchair, Mr. Stewart further explained that we were also waiting on the warden of the "Walls" to arrive.

A guard arrived with a wheelchair and placed it on the inside of the prison bars so that Wayne could use it as he entered through the locked steel door. A stocky man dressed in a brown suit, white shirt, brown tie, western hat and boots entered the foyer. He produced his I.D. for the guard, who said, "Good evening, Warden." Warden Neill Hodges had arrived. The steel door opened and everyone entered the prison. The heavy metal bar door closed with a loud clang. The witnesses were people who had just given up their freedom to witness justice.

Bill held the wheelchair handles as Wayne took a seat. Bill and Wayne took the elevator to the second floor while everyone else climbed the stairs. As the elevator door opened, Mr. Stewart escorted everyone to the victim's assistance personnel offices and counseling room. Everyone was offered a seat and in the next fifteen minutes, three more victim's assistance staff counselors and other TDCJ personnel filtered into the large lounge room. The day became an afternoon of "hurry-up-and-wait." Bill walked to the window. Yellow DO NOT CROSS tape was strung across the street that runs in front of the prison and extra guards could be seen. On the other side of the tape, five anti-capital punishment protestors had gathered. They were singing Christian hymns and holding anti-execution signs. It was 5:30 p.m.

Male and female guards arrived at the lounge room. Rex's time was drawing closer and closer. Both male and female witnesses were taken into the outer hallway and searched. With this task completed, it was time to move again. Bill rolled Wayne to the elevator while everyone else took the stairway back to the first floor. It was 5:50 p.m.

Mr. Stewart and a guard escorted the victim's witnesses to the prison's visitation room. The long row of about thirty visitation stalls with their plexi-glass windows and talking phones on either side of the glass could be seen. Bill heard a noise and looked behind his group to see another group of witnesses enter the visitation room. It was the members of the media who had been selected to view the execution. Davis recognized his friend Bill Leger, news anchor for Beaumont's KFDM Channel-6 TV, who had requested and been given permission to be one of the media witnesses. The media witnesses stayed at one end of the visitation room while the victim witnesses stayed at the other end. A door in the visitation room that lead to an inner courtyard was suddenly unlocked and opened. The outside guard asked one of the guards with the witnesses if everyone was ready. Following an affirmative nod, everyone was escorted through the door and along the sidewalk. All executions in Texas must take place any time after 6:00 p.m. on the date mandated on the death warrant. It was 6:02 p.m.

Everyone maintained a single-file as they walked along the narrow sidewalk through a courtyard. Another door was opened and another part of the building was entered. A few steps into the building and everyone walked through another door. The room was dark and narrow. Straight ahead was a large window with ran the width of the ten-foot-wide room. The witnesses eased up to the glass. Bill pushed Wayne's wheelchair to the left side of the window. Mike's sister stood next to the wheelchair. To her right stood Mike's wife and Mike stood at the right corner of the glass. Bill stood directly behind Mike's sister. TDCJ crime victim's personnel and guards stood behind the victim's witnesses and news media witnesses stood in the rear of the room. The room was lit with light coming through the glass. The room on the other side of the glass was the Texas death chamber. As Bill looked over the top of Mike's sister's head, Bill saw Rex Powell for the first time in twelve years. Rex had not changed much. His hair was grayer. His face was the same. Rex was lying on a gurney. He was wearing clean blue prison clothes. A pillow was under his head and both arms were strapped to arm rests slightly away from his body. His hands and arms were heavily wrapped with padding and ace bandages from beyond his fingertips to above the elbows. This was to hide his fingertips from any involuntary twitching as death occurred and to hide the intravenous needles and tubes that would deliver a lethal dose of drugs to Rex's body in a few short minutes. Two leather straps held Rex's legs in place as well as another leather strap across his chest. It was 6:08 p.m.

The death chamber was painted a mint green. There was a two-way mirror on the far right side of the room. The lethal dose of serum and the person to start the flow of drugs stood out of sight behind the mirror. The gurney was situated parallel to the glass window. The wall to the right in the victim's witness room separated that room from the room for Rex's witnesses. Rex's head was closest to his witnesses. Warden Hodges was standing with his back to the victim's witness window. A clergyman for Rex stood near his feet. A microphone hung several inches above Rex's head.

A door directly across the gurney from Warden Hodges opened. A guard took one step inside the death chamber and said, "Warden, you may proceed." Taking one step backward, the guard exited the room and closed the door. "Do you have any last words?" the Warden asked Rex.

This was Rex's opportunity to bare his soul. There was no need to hide his vicious secrets anymore. There was no need to take his apology to the grave. Death was imminent. There would be no other chance to make amends. All he had to do was turn his head to the right, look Mike Van Winkle in the eyes and say "I'm sorry." But he didn't. All he said was "I'm ready for the final blessing." It was 6:10 p.m.

Some form of communication took place between Warden Hodges and the person behind the two-way mirror. No one but those two knew what the Warden's "sign" was, but with Rex's statement over, it was time for the execution to begin. Rex did not speak again verbally. But he did begin to lip sync the words "I love you" over and over while continuously looking at his wife. Suddenly his eyes closed. Sodium thiopental, the first of three drugs for the execution was taking effect and sedating Rex.

About fifteen seconds after closing his eyes, Rex's chest heaved three huge gasps for breath. The second drug, pancuronium bromide, had entered Rex's veins. This drug is a muscle relaxant and was collapsing Rex's diaphragm and lungs. Even though there were no visible signs of the third drug being administered, Mr. Stewart had advised in his briefing that after Rex's breathing stopped, potassium chloride, used to stop the heart, would be the last drug administered to Rex. Bill constantly watched Rex's chest. It had stopped. There was no doubt the third drug was being administered. It was over. No one moved. Everyone in the victim's witness room stared at the lifeless form for what seemed like eternity. Bill looked upon the man hoping he had made peace with God, yet knowing Rex had not seized the moment to make peace with mankind. The warden and clergyman continued to gaze upon Rex's body. Crying could be heard from the other room. It was 6:12 p.m.

Approximately five minutes lapsed and the door across the gurney from the warden opened again. A doctor entered the room. He held a stethoscope to Rex's body. A few more seconds passed and the doctor pronounced Rex dead. The potassium chloride had done its job. Warden Hodges took the sheet that covered Rex's body up to his abdomen and pulled it over his head. A lone train whistle could be heard in the distant background. It was 6:17 p.m.

The victim's witnesses and media witnesses were ushered from the viewing room. Everyone was escorted back to the second floor lounge for a short debriefing before going their separate ways. Bill helped Wayne out of the prison and to his waiting vehicle. The two friends bade their goodbyes with a promise to keep in touch. Both commented they wished their friend Bill Tatum could have been there. Bill turned from Wayne's car to see Mary waiting for him in the parking lot. Bill Leger came out of the media room and interviewed Bill, getting his thoughts on the execution for the 10:00 p.m. news. Leger then left Huntsville, hurrying to make it back to Beaumont in time for the late night news.

Bill and Mary went to a local restaurant for supper. His mind went over and over not only the events of the evening, but the events going back to October 6, 1990. Rex had simply closed his eyes, never to awaken again. Bill pictured Falyssa's tortured face as Rex pulled the rope around her neck tighter and tighter as he viciously raped her innocent little body. He pictured the little girl as tears stained her cheeks and she gasped for breath. The State of Texas had finally carried out its punishment to Rex Powell. Yet was there really justice?

Rex Powell was executed six days shy of the twelfth anniversary of Falyssa's kidnapping, rape, and murder. He spent approximately nine months in the Newton County Jail at a cost of approximately $40.00 per day. Rex was transferred to death row the day after his trial and spent approximately eleven years and four months on death row at a cost of $61.58 per day. Rex's total time of incarceration cost the citizens of Newton County and the citizens of the State of Texas approximately $265,433. His execution cost $86.08. Rex was the twenty-ninth death row inmate to be put to death in Texas in 2002. The average stay on death row is 10.49 years. Rex exceeded that time by approximately one year.

A person once commented to Bill Davis, "Rex Powell was allowed to live longer on death row than he allowed Falyssa to live on this earth." What a terrible but true comparison. There are those people who say the death penalty is not a deterrent to crime. Rex's execution guaranteed that he would never harm or molest anyone ever again. Rex's execution gave some form of closure to Elaine, Joe, Shonna, and Mike. And yet there is never complete closure. Falyssa was robbed of the opportunity to have boyfriends, to go on dates, to go to the prom, to graduate from high school and college, to get married, to have children. Those close to her were denied the opportunity to go shopping for prom dresses, to attend graduations, to attend weddings, to be the grandparents or the aunt of Falyssa's children.

Falyssa was still so innocent, yet so dead.

God rest her soul.

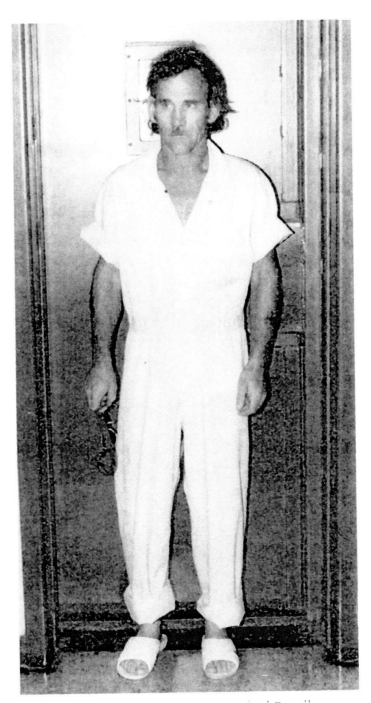
Condemned murderer James Rexford Powell.

CHAPTER TWENTY

A THEORY

(** **NOTE: Rex Powell never talked to the authorities about his involvement with Falyssa's kidnapping, rape, and murder except for his affidavit given on October 7, 1990. His pertinent statements on that affidavit were proven to be a lie. The author's aim in this chapter is to recount what investigators believe really happened on October 6, 1990. This theory is based on facts uncovered during the investigation, and on the profiles of those who commit such unspeakable crimes.)**

Rex Powell did not wake up on the morning of October 6, 1990, with the idea or the urge to kidnap, rape, and murder a little girl.

After seeing his wife off to work, he got in his motor home and headed to Old Time Trade Days weekend at Larry's Antique Mall. He arrived at 8:00 a.m. and parked his motor home in the main parking lot. He wandered around looking at the many items for sale. Occasionally, he stopped and visited with people he knew. Their conversation was general and light-hearted.

Some time between 8:00 and 9:00 a.m., Rex ambled by Joe Langley's booth and stopped to visit. Falyssa walked outside their camper. It had begun to rain, and Falyssa was complaining that Joe and Elaine had forgotten to bring milk for her cereal and she was having to eat it dry. She spoke to Rex, who returned her greeting.

In his deviant mind as Rex watched Falyssa, he probably began to imagine what it would be like to have sex with her. It's very possible that he had thought about it several times in the past. His twisted mind wandered to her blossoming puberty. Then Falyssa derailed his fantasy. She smiled ever so delightfully and told Rex about her boyfriend. She showed him his picture. Rex looked at the boy's picture and tried to remain calm and congenial. But Joe Langley had seen Rex's mood change abruptly. Rex's sexual fantasy had turned into a nightmare. All he could think about was this boy having Falyssa. A few minutes later he left. He pretended to be looking at items other people had on display but his thoughts were still on Falyssa.

Rex was an opportunist. He was still not thinking of something so bold as kidnapping Falyssa. But the thought of that boy and girl in his fantasy just wouldn't go away.

A few minutes after 10:00 a.m., Rex saw Falyssa again among hundreds of people. Yet to him they were alone. A sick part of his mind told him if the opportunity arose to have her, seize it. And then, it happened. Falyssa smiled and said, "Hi." A simple moment, but just enough to push Rex over the edge.

Falyssa had been taught not to go anywhere without permission. Rex had probably observed this parental discipline over the previous year or so that he'd known Falyssa and her parents. He knew he would need a scheme to lure her inside his motor home.

Rex collected fruit jars. Investigators speculated that he told Falyssa that her mom had bought some fruit jars from him. He may have told her that he was going to leave, asking Falyssa if she would save him a trip by accompanying him to his motor home to get the jars. He may have even mentioned that little Falyssa's favor would really help his bad back. Always wanting to do things for her beloved mother, Falyssa readily agreed.

As Rex and Falyssa approached his motor home, his mind was racing. If she stood at the door and refused to enter he would give her a couple of jars. If he could lure her inside, he would have her alone to carry out his deviant scheme. Rex unlocked the motor home and went inside.

As Falyssa stood outside the door Rex may have asked her to come inside and help him retrieve the jars. She'd known Rex for a year. He'd always been a nice man. She may have been reluctant to enter the vehicle, but thinking she was doing a good deed for her mom, she entered the vehicle unaware. Rex may have asked her to reach up on a shelf or into a cabinet, anything to get her to turn her back. In the blink of an eye Rex passed the point of no return. He hit Falyssa on the head with a blunt instrument, knocking her unconscious. He quickly grabbed some rope and tied her hands and ankles. He stuffed a washcloth into her mouth just far enough to prevent her from crying out for someone, anyone, to rescue her.

Rex realized he couldn't just leave. He needed an alibi. He exited the motor home and double-checked to make sure the door was locked. He walked back to the vendor area and spotted Falyssa's step-dad. Rex walked up to Joe and showed him a little ink well that he claimed to have bought. He appeared calm as he told Joe goodbye and that he'd see him next month. Joe watched the "Mayor of Mauriceville" walk to his motor home in the parking lot, never suspecting Falyssa was in the vehicle. Joe watched as Rex's white motor home exited the parking lot and drove out of sight on the Eastex Freeway service road.

Like a wolf that carries its prey to its den, Rex headed as straight and as fast as he could to the wooded area he knew well in western Beauregard Parish, Louisiana. He had hunted this area since he was a little boy. The back of his father-in-law's property butted up to these woods. The motor home would only go about fifty mph., making the ninety-mile trip in about two hours.

Unexpectedly, Falyssa regained consciousness. Her mouth was dry and she could hardly swallow. She realized something was in her mouth. Her hands and her ankles were hurting. She saw the bindings. She began to cry, but no sound came out. She could feel the vibrations and rocking of the vehicle. She saw the person driving. She wondered why Rex wasn't helping her. He was her friend. At some point, Rex turned around and saw that the girl was awake and alert. The look on his face made her realize he was not a nice man, but her captor.

As Rex crossed over the Sabine River Bridge into Louisiana, he gradually slowed the motor home. A quarter-mile later he turned right onto an old logging road. A few hundred yards later, he stopped the vehicle. The wolf had arrived at his den.

Rex grabbed another piece of rope and tied a slip knot in it as he placed it around Falyssa's neck. He wanted to make sure he had complete control of her before he cut the ropes loose from her ankles so he could get her legs apart. The tears streaming down Falyssa's cheeks in pure, blind, unmitigated fear probably heightened his sinister erotic pleasure. He cut the ropes around her ankles keeping the rope around her neck taut enough to keep her still. Adding to her fear and his pleasure, he removed her shorts and panties.

As he undressed himself, he might have told her, as sex offenders often do, that she was going to see what it was like to be with a man. He mounted her and penetrated the very being of her soul. The pain was excruciating but her cries fell on deaf ears. Rex forced himself into her like an animal gone mad. As he got closer to climax he pulled the rope tighter around her little neck. Reaching the peak of his unthinkable act, he jerked on the rope and Falyssa's gasping stopped.

Rex had no intention of hauling this dead girl around in his vehicle; he needed to find a shallow grave in this desolate area. Maybe he intended to dump her body in a ravine. At that moment, as if by Divine intervention, it started to rain - not a shower, but a fierce thunderstorm.

On this first weekend day of squirrel season in Texas and Louisiana, the woods were full of hunters. As the rain poured, hunters began to appear out of nowhere. Rex worried about getting his heavy vehicle stuck on the old logging road. He put Falyssa's underwear and shorts back on her. Except for the ropes, Falyssa looked like a napping child.

Rex drove back to Hwy. 190, turning right into the path of oncoming traffic.

He entered Bon Wier and turned onto Hwy. 1416. Rex's friend, Waymon Jacks, saw Rex make the turn through his rear view *mirror. It was 1:30 p.m.*

Desperate by now to dispose of Falyssa's body, Rex headed west passing Roderick Nelson on his way home from squirrel hunting. Rex turned right onto what he thought was Fox Hunter Road.

It took him a few minutes to realize he had not gone far enough on Hwy. 2460 to reach Fox Hunter Road. From her front porch, Mary Jenkins saw Rex. He sat at the dead-end of her road, revving the engine to the motor home while he tried to decide which way to turn. This was not working out like he'd figured.

He turned around on Jenkins' Road, drove back to Hwy. 2460 and turned west. About one-quarter-mile farther west he turned onto Fox Hunter Road. He drove past Bill Aycock and friends playing horseshoes. As he tried to find a side road that would support the weight of his vehicle, he again ran into problems. All of the side roads were too wet and too soft to take a chance of driving on them. It must have seemed like forever for Rex to travel the seventeen-mile-long road in his cumbersome vehicle. He may even have stopped beside some of the side roads to check their firmness before driving on. At the intersection of Fox Hunter Road and Hwy. 363, he sat at the stop sign trying to figure out where he could dump Falyssa's body. He couldn't turn right on Hwy. 363. That would cause him to drive past Judge Satterwhite's store and people there knew his vehicle. This may have even been when Rex got the idea to use the judge as an alibi. He turned left and headed west, then it struck him: there was one place he could dump the child's body and not even have to get out of the motor home -- under Cow Creek Bridge.

Rex drove through the community of Bleakwood. Turning left on Hwy. 87, he drove about half an hour to Hwy. 1416. He could see Cow Creek Bridge a quarter-mile away. He turned left to drive down the north embankment of the bridge. He was sure no one had seen him. Hopefully, no one would be under the bridge.

Rex saw the huge mud puddle at the end of the asphalt ramp. He couldn't back up the ramp, so he slammed the accelerator to the floor. Finally, the vehicle was on solid ground.

Rex drove under the bridge and stopped. He looked around to make sure no one was there. He grabbed the rope around Falyssa's neck and dragged her across the plywood floor to the rear door of the vehicle. Making sure that he was still alone, he opened the back door and jerked the rope hard enough to pull Falyssa's body out. He tossed her head band and the extra rope into a nearby bush. Within a matter of seconds he was back in the driver's seat. As he fled, the air conditioner cowling struck the underside of the bridge. He slammed on the brakes and got out to see what had caused the terrible racket. Back inside, Rex eased the vehicle out from under the bridge. He climbed the embankment and drove onto the highway, again into the path of an oncoming truck -- Louis Thompson and the Hopkins brothers.

Rex headed toward Bon Wier. With the body disposed, it was time to further develop his alibi. In Bon Wier, Rex turned left onto Hwy. 363. Minutes later he drove into the parking lot of Judge Satterwhite's store and parked near the back door. He was feeling pretty confident as he entered the auction area and saw the justice of the peace. Why shouldn't he? He had encountered lots of problems in getting rid of Falyssa's body and had overcome them all. After visiting with the judge, Rex headed home.

Rex headed west from Judge Satterwhite's store on Hwy. 363 past the intersection of Hwy. 363 and Fox Hunter Road.

In Kirbyville, he turned left onto Hwy. 96 and drove south through town. David Jacks spotted Rex and his motor home as he and his sisters drove north on the same highway.

An hour or so later Rex pulled into his own driveway. As he parked his vehicle, he noticed all the cars at his neighbor's house across the street. He didn't know those people and he had Judge Satterwhite as an alibi. But Rex thought another alibi certainly couldn't hurt.

He sauntered across the street and introduced himself to the two men sitting on the front porch. After carrying on small talk for a few minutes and drinking one of Elton Gish's beers, Rex bade the men a good day and ambled back across the street. He had satisfied his sexual desires, had felt that fantastic feeling of power, had discarded Falyssa's body, and had developed not one, but two good alibis.

Rex saw the lead story on the evening 6:00 news. The conclusion of the news story caught his attention: No suspects were in custody.

But Rex's mood would change in less than twenty-four hours. John Dean would call his house and ask him about being a minor witness in the investigation. If Rex had initiated the phone call, he might have continued to be in control. He would have had everything planned that he wanted to say. But he was caught off-guard. He panicked.

Falyssa Van Winkle had been so young, so full of energy. Her vitality had been a ray of sunshine to the many lives she had touched.

In contrast, Rex Powell's life had been a devastating nightmare to the lives he had touched. His actions had brought heartache and sorrow to many, and within days, his personal nightmare would become reality.

Aerial photography of Larry's Antique Mall during Old Time Trade Days, taken a few months before the crime. Studying an enlargement of this photo on display inside the building, Sgt. Bill Davis spotted Rex Powell's motor home in the parking lot, positioned near Falyssa's family's vending booth.

BILL DAVIS SEMINARS

CHILD ABUSE: A NATIONAL EPIDEMIC*

Bill takes you on an emotional roller coaster ride, laughing one minute and crying the next with his inspired presentation about crimes against the most innocent element of society – our children. Using more than 400 slides, he talks about physical, neglectful, emotional, and sexual abuses to children. The program, which includes a review of positive parenting skills, is adapted to high school and adult audiences as a four-hour lecture or an eight-hour seminar. It's a program you can't say you enjoyed, but it's one you'll never forget. The information you receive just might save a child's life.

CHILD SAFETY: FIRST & FOREVER WITH OFFICER BILL

When it's time to teach safety to children, Sgt. Davis becomes "Officer Bill" to his little friends. Officer Bill's 30-minute program for preschool and elementary children addresses bicycle safety, traffic signs, and seat belts. Officer Bill reinforces their right to say NO to drugs and crime. Finally, he deals with the sensitive issue of "good touches" and "bad touches," and the "UH-OH" touch in a very sensitive and understanding manner. Officer Bill's interaction with children keeps their attention at a constant high level. (This program is available on DVD through corporate sponsorship or individual purchase.)

SEX AND THE LAW

Most adults are reluctant to talk to teenagers about sex. Bill's program with teenagers is one class-period long and is filled with audience interaction. His 90-minute program IS NOT a sex eduation program. Very candidly and professionally, he discusses the various criminal laws dealing with sexual encounters that relate to young adults. Bill also addresses civil laws dealing with pregnancy, paternity suits, child support, and rights of the mother, father, and child. The program is filled with laughter, anxiousness, and undivided attention from his audience.

SEXUAL ABUSE: IDENTIFICATION AND REPORTING

Sgt. Davis has investigated more than 7,000 child abuse and sex-crime cases. In this presentation, he discusses the elements of some of the most-often used criminal statutes dealing with sex crimes. Sgt. Davis discusses rape and child sexual abuse including pedophilia and incest.

PERSONAL SAFETY: A FACT OF LIFE*

More often in modern society, our work takes us out of the safety and security of our homes and offices into places and situations that can put our safety at risk. These include social service case workers, home nurses, real estate agents, volunteers, sales people, and others whose everyday leisure pursuits - jogging, shopping, camping - place them in the path of potential criminal activity. In this 90-minute presentation, Sgt. Davis presents some common-sense ideas and defensive tactics to help both men and women maintain a higher level of awareness and preparedness while working to keep others safe.

Booking Information

Contact: Sgt. Bill Davis

Home: (409) 866-0490
Cell: (409) 781-5726
Fax: (409) 866-0720

Email: bill@takingcareofchildren.net

Address: 8820 Blaylock Lane, Beaumont, Texas 77707

*continuing education credits available

imperfect love

imperfect justice

Written by
BILL DAVIS
The Police Detective Who Investigated The Crime

IMPERFECT LOVE ~ IMPERFECT JUSTICE

By: Bill Davis
The Police Detective Who Investigated The Crime

Martha returned home from taking her fourteen-year-old son, Luke, to evening Bible study at church. She stopped by the store and picked up a few groceries and needed to get the perishables into the refrigerator. Martha entered her home and put the groceries in the foyer. Her need to use the bathroom was urgent. Martha began ascending the steps to the second floor where the bathroom was located. She was halfway up the stairs when her husband, Steve, suddenly appeared from the bathroom wearing only his boxer shorts. He quickly began descending the stairs. As they passed one another, Martha noticed the light was on in the bathroom and she mechanically called out, "Next!" It was a habit the family adopted as their bathroom door for the time being was a black plastic curtain, and it served as their only privacy while in the bathroom. "I'm almost dressed, I'm hurrying," was the response she heard from the soft voice she recognized as that of her eleven-year-old daughter. As Martha climbed the last few steps, Victoria came into view. She was sitting on the commode seat clad in only a white bra and a pair of cotton panties. Fear gripped Martha as she saw her little girl staring at the floor, refusing to meet her mother's gaze. Martha's throat had a huge lump in it as her voice quivered, "What's going on here, Victoria?"

Martha was fighting the realization that Victoria's silence was becoming the answer she did not want to hear. Martha's world quickly turned upside down that fateful night. Her worst fear became reality. Her daughter had been molested by her own father. For Victoria, it was a relief that the secret was finally out. The molestation had been going on as far back as she could remember. Martha had two children to protect. What should she do? Where should she go?

Victoria's story is true. Names and places have been changed to protect the innocent people involved in her story. This story is much like numerous others, stories of child sexual abuse victims and survivors. It is a story that people in our society do not want to hear, nor believe, but one that needs to be told.

Victoria's police investigator, Sgt. Bill Davis, investigated thousands of child abuse and sex crimes cases in his thirty-six year police career with the Beaumont, Texas Police Department. This case would become one of his most unusual and complex investigations. For this reason, Sgt. Davis chose this investigation to be the subject of his second true crime novel. Travel with Sgt. Davis through several Southeast Texas counties, to a West Texas mountain top, and into the heart of a little girl. Sit in the jury box as the trial unfolds and hear candid testimony of how a master manipulator managed to victimize his daughter for over seven years. You won't be able to put this book down until the last page is read.

IMPERFECT LOVE ~ IMPERFECT JUSTICE
ISBN: 978-0-9850403-7-6

CPSIA information can be obtained
at www.ICGtesting.com
Printed in the USA
LVOW07s2340071017
551569LV00001B/1/P